TO BECOME
ONE

BY CHRIS SEAY & CHAD KARGER

[RELEVANTBOOKS]

Published by Relevant Books
A division of Relevant Media Group, Inc.

www.relevantbooks.com
www.relevantmediagroup.com

© 2004 by Relevant Media Group

Design: Relevant Solutions
www.relevant-solutions.com
Cover design by Aaron Martin
Interior design by Matt Crow

Relevant Books is a registered trademark of Relevant Media Group, Inc., and is
registered in the U.S. Patent and Trademark Office.

For information:
RELEVANT MEDIA GROUP, INC.
POST OFFICE BOX 951127
LAKE MARY, FL 32795
407-333-7152

Library of Congress Control Number: 2003096208
International Standard Book Number: 0-9729276-1-1

04 05 06 07 9 8 7 6 5 4 3 2 1

Printed in the United States of America

From Chris:

To Lisa, thanks for making life a beautiful journey!

From Chad:

For Meeka, the love of my life and whose voice is embedded in my own ... thanks for learning with me.

ACKNOWLEDGMENTS

From Chris:

For Lisa, Hanna, Trinity, and my son Solomon you all make my life sweet. Mom, Dad, Brian, Amy, Jen, Rusty, Robbie, Liz, Jessica, Noni, Papa, Terry, Sharon, Lisa, Eddie, Sam, Ruth, Sammy, Hannah, Pam, and Bob— thank you for the important part you play in our life!

To Ecclesia and the elders (Chad, Robbie, Justin, Paul, and Tim) staff (Tyndall, Christy, Jennifer, Tom), for being the kind of community that inspires and encourages this kind of reflection and creation. To Eugene Peterson for The Message. You have given us a beautiful gift. Cara Davis, my editor, I pray God's richest blessings on your new union—Thank you. All of my gratitude to Chad Karger, who is an extraordinary friend and source of good counsel.

To West End Baptist Church, Emergent, Youth Specialties, BGCT, The Baptist Standard, Baylor University, Art and Soul, Houston Astros, and our friends at the Houstonian.

From Chad:

Thanks Meeka, Reece, Noah, and Aimee for welcoming me home, our playground and oasis, at the end of each day. Meeka, I can't believe it's been nearly fifteen years since I illegally kissed you in the Chalet. I love you. Reece, you are creative and strong. Noah, you are brave and true. Aimee, you are beautiful and mischievous.

I also would like to thank Mom and Dad, who have weathered storms that would have wrecked a weaker marriage. You have loved us well. I'd also like to thank my sister, Kim, and her family for their love and support and honesty. Thanks Nanny and Papa Bill and Grandma and Papa. Betty and Glen, you have welcomed me into your family as though I was one of your own. I'm forever grateful for your blessing in our marriage. To Kris, Don, Curt, Nicky, and Leif, I always enjoy time with you and am appreciative for your support and encouragement.

Richard, Mack, Phil, and Jerry, what could I say to you that would even come close to the gratitude I feel in my heart? Your camaraderie has been a taste of God in this world for me. I am indebted to you and your wives for any wisdom in these pages. Chris, thanks for going down this and many other roads with me. It is a privilege to work alongside you; God's calling burns bright and intense in your life.

Thanks Ecclesia. You are truly an inspiration to us wherever we go and whatever we do. Thanks to Justin,

Paul, and Robbie for your prayers and support. Thanks
for helping to keep the fire burning at home, Tyndall and
Andrea. To the deacons who serve tirelessly within our
faith family, I pray that you will find more in your life with
God than you have given away.

Finally, thanks Cara for your patience in this project. I
know it wasn't easy. I pray that God would richly bless you
as you enter into marriage.

CONTENTS

INTRODUCTION

The Creator looked toward man and saw the beauty of His creation, but knew that it was not good for man to be alone. Marriage is about joining together in a way that means you will never again be alone. It sounds simple, but the reality is that many husbands and wives live more like disconnected roommates. Even being roommates is difficult, right? Have you chosen to live with a friend thinking you would get along cheerily, only to find your friendship turned into a feud leading inevitably to some kind of fight-to-the-death cage match?

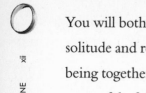

You will both require a life balanced with times of solitude and reflection—marriage is not about always being together. It is about always be cognizant and respectful of the other when you are in separate places. I (Chris) enjoy time spent in solitude—there is nothing better to me than going to a movie all by myself. There are many things that Lisa and I enjoy doing alone or with other friends, but I now live with a constant sense of her presence and importance in my life.

If you are turning these pages, it's likely you are either married or contemplating nuptials, and you are increasing your chances of success because you care enough to read a book that will prompt you toward discussion. Dive into this book passionately. Feel free to disagree with us or with one another—but chart a course that will bring the two of you together building a family on a foundation of trust, faith, and love. I love marriage and highly recommend it to everyone, but let me be clear—it is not easy. Nothing capable of bringing so much joy, pleasure, and fulfillment ever is.

The time will come, or likely already has, when romance fizzles and the butterflies in your stomach flutter away, leaving a whirlwind of emotions and experiences that are sometimes good and often painful. Don't get married because you have nothing better to do, and don't take your vows lightly. Give everything you have to the success of this sacred union. If you do, the joy you find in one another will be incomparable. If it is possible that you will put vocational success, friends, or other family members before your spouse—don't proceed. Your vows don't allow for any other earthly allegiances to supersede this union. In fact, your pledge is to literally lose yourself in one another. The Bible describes it as a miraculous merger where "Two Become One."

Lisa and I had a whirlwind romance. We met in the Garden of the Gods, literally in

THIS WAS AN INCREDIBLE CEL-EBRATION. AT THE AGE OF THIRTY-TWO, I HAD FOUND THE MAN I WOULD SLEEP NEXT TO THE REST OF MY LIFE. IT FELT REALLY GOOD. —LISA SEAY

a castle nuzzled between massive mountains in Colorado Springs. I was speaking at a conference, and in this sea of clergy, there was an intelligent woman with a captivating beauty who caught my attention and soon my heart. We have contradicting versions of the story (she says I was an overt flirt, and I say she manhandled her way into situations where we could be together, but the truth

is, we were taken with one another almost instantly.)
Within weeks I was visiting her in Chicago, and before
two months had passed, we were engaged. I flew to
Chicago as a surprise, and in a quiet piano bar, I asked
her to be my "true companion." We were elated; we
celebrated and devoured large platters of crab legs. I'll
never forget the sensation of complete and unrestrained
joy. Heaven should be so good.

Fast-forward one year, Lisa and I have been married for
more than six months. We have traveled to wonderful
cities, honeymooned in the Caribbean, and set up our
home together in a cozy two-bedroom bungalow. But
life has not been easy, and resentment is festering. In a
moment of deep calm, Lisa articulates the depth of our
problems: "I am so angry with you, that I have awful
thoughts like I wish you were dead." I freeze. My body
wants to cry, but shuts down instead. Did my bride just
say she thought life would be easier without me? I could
either reel from the pain of her words, or get ready to
be gut wrenchingly honest and take our relationship to
a new level. Our journey to oneness during the second
half of our first year of marriage was painful. We aired
our angst, dirty laundry, and quarrels to a small group of

people who loved us and prayed for us. Healing was slow but steady.

Lisa and I are both very strong-willed and exceedingly independent. Forsaking our own desires, beliefs, and opinions did not come easy. We wanted to have our cake and eat it too and to enjoy the beauty of marital bliss without the self-sacrifice that makes it possible. Our plan was a failure, so we began a new path that involved total self-disclosure and the marriage of our hearts. Commitment sustained us through the hard times and opened the doors to make us better people, passionate lovers of God, and best friends.

MEEKA AND I (CHAD) MET IN COLORADO TOO. WE WERE YOUNG BUT HAD COLLECTED OUR SHARE OF BROKEN HEARTS. GOING VERY SLOW AND FORGING A FRIENDSHIP WAS VERY IMPORTANT TO US. OUR FEELINGS FOR EACH OTHER WERE STRONG; WE KNEW THIS RELATIONSHIP WOULD GO MUCH TOO FAST IF WE WEREN'T ON GUARD.
—CHAD KARGER

The wonders of marriage are simple. In a glance, kiss, or touch of her hand, I am welcomed into a world of security and love. At the end of a hectic and exhausting day, I anticipate the serene joy of crawling into bed with my wife. No matter what had or hadn't happened, no matter the disappointment or anticipation, lying next to her, feeling her naked feet and legs under the covers is like touching the eternal rhythms in a river somewhere in heaven.

Lisa and I have been married seven years, Chad and Meeka thirteen, but we are not marriage experts. This book is a collection of our experiences as husbands and pastors making mistakes and walking through dark roads with many others. Lisa spent many years as a marriage and family counselor. She and Meeka will add an honest and poignant voice to this book through sidebars that give you a sense of their perspective and insight. As you journey toward the altar, we are grateful to be able to walk a part of that path with you.

MEEKA AND I SPENT THE FIRST FIVE YEARS OF OUR MARRIAGE GETTING (OR STRUGGLING) TO KNOW ONE ANOTHER. WE MISSED OUT ON THE TWENTYSOMETHING, COLLEGE-LIFE RITE OF PASSAGE SO ESTEEMED IN OUR NORTH AMERICAN CULTURE. ON THE OTHER HAND, WE BUILT A LIFE TOGETHER AND MISSED A LOT OF STRUGGLES INVOLVED IN SHARING LIFE THAT PEOPLE FACE WHO MARRY AFTER THAT PASSAGE. MEEKA AND I ARE LIVING PROOF OF MARRIAGE'S ENIGMATIC NATURE. A HEALTHY MARRIAGE DISRUPTS FORMULAS AND SYSTEMS FOR SUCCESS. IT IS A PRACTICAL ENDEAVOR AS MUCH AS IT IS A MYSTERY LIVED IN REAL LIFE. IT HAS GOD'S NAME WRITTEN ALL OVER IT. —CK

Chad's grandfather recently passed away. Right up
until he breathed his last, Nanny and Papa Bill were
kissing and calling each other names like two teenagers
in love. He was ninety-five. Both Chad and I can tell
stories of hard work and raw passion that shaped our
parents' relationships. I pray that the statistics will not
be true for those who read these pages. I pray that your
commitment to one another sustains you when romance
and feelings fail you. May we all become doting senior
citizens absorbed by the love of our lifelong sweethearts.

All of that is to simply say that I approach the themes
in this book with humility; I am deeply aware of the
fact that my relationship with Lisa still finds me a
selfish and arrogant man at times. Walk with us to the
caldron of commitment and know that any wisdom or
understanding that is written on these pages comes from
a growing fear within the authors. The one, true God is
to be feared above all else in this life. More than divorce
or infidelity, unruly kids and/or debt, God should hold
our vision like a father holds his bewildered, hopeful
child's attention.

Scripture promises that the fear of God leads to wisdom.

The fear of anything or anyone else leaves us isolated, wounded, and disillusioned. The difference is that the fear of God is the place of worship, and the fear of anything else is the beginning of idolatry. So moving together into a place of reverence puts all our other desires in perspective. In that space we are free from lust, materialism, ego, hedonism, and addiction.

"Stay" is one my favorite songs we sing at Ecclesia. Robbie Seay (my brother and our worship pastor) has captured what I believe to be a very real and familiar place for a couple, a humble, contrite, confident place of worship. Much like the disciples in the Gospel of John, we remain insecure of God's love and continued presence in our lives.

> *Don't leave this place*
> *don't leave this place*
> *we are scared that we'll be left here all alone*
> *so we fall down on our faces*
> *You are the sunlight in our darkness*
> *You are the truth among our lying*
> *You are the life within our graves*
> *don't leave this place*

Holy Spirit stay, stay
Take our pride and exchange it for Your grace
take our will and exchange it for Your way
stay

Just as Christ promised to "never leave us," your vows to one another are an eternal covenant. I pray that you develop the resolve to press into the inevitable trials and joys that await you. The best advice we can give you is to *stay* present with one another. We humbly submit the following for your prayerful consideration.

"Our sense of emptiness is thus not accidental, nor is it a spurious and meaningless irritation. It is a fundamental clue to our origin, purpose, and destiny."

—Alister McGrath, *The Unknown God*

1. A PATH TO MATRIMONY

Too many Christians have planted their relationships on stagnant ground. Because we have not been given many guides on life, faith, and family, many of us are easily converted by the plethora of formulaic dating books on the market. Dating philosophies are among the most confusing and controversial teachings in faith circles. If you are in the "courtship" crew or the "extended engagement" gang, hold your philosophy loosely and realize it is just that, your philosophy.

Dating is a cultural construct that has morphed over the course of time. Typically, there are two fatal flaws when it comes to marriage, and they relate to extremism in two areas: dating philosophy and spouse selection.

Dating Philosophy

1. A blinding focus on finding Mr. or Mrs. Right that does not allow for friendship to blossom. Casual and pleasurable companionship is an important part of friendship and dating.

2. A "live in the moment" philosophy that makes the most of fun while ignoring the future and never considering marriage and commitment.

Spouse Selection

1. Choosing a spouse totally based on your own criteria and refusing to seek wisdom from family, elders, and friends.

2. The historical practice of a family selecting a spouse with no consideration of an individual's personal preference.

OBVIOUSLY THE EMPHASIS ON PURITY AND INTEGRITY IN RELATIONSHIP IS CRITICAL. IT NEEDS TO BE TALKED ABOUT. THE PROBLEM ARISES WHEN THE BOOKS AND ARMCHAIR EXPERTS BEGIN TO OFFER PRESCRIPTIONS INSTEAD OF PRINCIPLES. TELL YOUR STORY, WITH ITS SUCCESSES AND FAILURES. BUT STOP TRYING TO WRITE A FOOLPROOF PLAN. READ THE SCRIPTURE AND LET IT SPEAK, AS IT DOES SO WELL, ABOUT WHAT PURITY IN LIFE AND INTEGRITY IN ALL RELATIONSHIPS LOOKS LIKE. DATING CANNOT BE A FORMULA. —CHAD KARGER

So avoid these extremes; moderation in all things is essential. Although rules are made to be broken, there are some important principles that should always guide our journey to find a partner for all of life. Regardless of our context and place in culture, we benefit from considering these timeless principles.

1) Community—Selecting a spouse in isolation is marital suicide; seek the counsel of the wisest people you know and listen to them. They will see things you don't and their help will be essential as you begin your family.

EVEN MORE IMPORTANT THAN WRITING SOMEONE OFF BECAUSE THEY COME FROM A SCREWED UP FAMILY IS HOW YOUR SPOUSE RELATES TO THEIR FAMILY. FIND CHANCES TO SEE HOW YOUR PARTNER RELATES TO YOUR FAMILY AND TALK ABOUT THE POTENTIAL PITFALLS. —LISA SEAY

2) Family—You don't marry a person; you marry a family. It's more than a cliché; it is true. You are selecting your children's grandparents, uncles, and role models, so do it thoughtfully.

3) Faith—If your Myers Briggs tests don't match up, ignore it, but if you don't share the same faith—bail!

As a single adult, these questions seem paramount:

"Where do I go to meet the right person? Is it wrong to date for fun? How can I fight off my sexual impulses?" The struggle is not that these questions are hard to answer, which they are, but that we are asking all the wrong questions.

We often sound like a spoiled child obsessed with what we do not have, unable to live in the moment and enjoy the room full of toys that already surround us. The hardest thing to do in life is to live in the moment, single or married, and take pleasure in our blessings. The beginning of our story is upset by God's ominous verdict that it is not good for "man to be alone," and all of us understanding a deep longing to have a partner. However, the Apostle Paul says it is "better not to marry." Is one right and the other wrong? No. We, like God, are made to live in community. But marriage is only one example of communal living. Whether your path leads to marriage or not, choose to live a full life marked by family, community, and contentment.

If I were to summarize a philosophy of dating and courtship, its essence would be found by understanding the fifth chapter of Matthew.

Dating, in whatever format you choose, should lead you to the most important questions in life. However, not many couples spend their Friday nights sharing a nice meal and discussing the intricacies of the Sermon on the Mount. So here goes, but be warned, these issues and questions are much more profound and important than, "How many kids do you want? or "Did you think you would marry a blond or brunette?" If you find compatibility based around the eternal issues raised in Matthew 5, your connection will outlast your youthful good looks and sustain you decades later.

READ TOGETHER AND DISCUSS:

Jesus said: "You're blessed when you're at the end of your rope. With less of you there is more of God and his rule."[1]

Anxiety, loneliness, and depression may be the tools in the hand of a loving Creator. If you feel backed in a corner—surrender. Talk to your partner about the darkest moments in your single life. When did you feel most alone? What did you do to get through it? Do you think marriage will be the solution to these problems?

How can both of you develop patterns of relying more on God when times are tough?

"You're blessed when you feel you've lost what is most dear to you. Only then can you be embraced by the One most dear to you."[2]

Loss, death, and despair give birth to a real neediness. Too often we live our lives with complete independence believing we do not truly need one another. Loss draws us into community—the kind needed in marriage. When have you experienced deep loss? And what would it look like to live life and marriage in that posture of humility and interdependence? How does that interdependence scare you?

"You're blessed when you're content with just who you are—no more, no less. That's the moment you find yourselves proud owners of everything that can't be bought."[3]

Dating is about putting your best foot forward; marriage is not. The first year of marriage is often a jarring reality. Your spouse will not always look, act, or smell their best.

Are you ready to love your spouse as the blinding light of marriage amplifies their faults? Discuss how you might journey together toward contentment with who you are, and who you are together. Can you see reality instead of who you long to be? The moment you experience the most profound expressions of love will likely be the times you are embraced in your flaws and imperfections.

"You're blessed when you've worked up a good appetite for God. He's food and drink in the best meal you'll ever eat."[4]

Intimacy with one another will not replace a hunger for the things of God. It is easy to become complacent. How will the two of you avoid a lazy spirituality? Are you aware of the other things you want and how badly you want them? Are they idols?

"You're blessed when you care. At the moment of being 'carefull,' you find yourselves cared for."[5]

Many advocate a me-first philosophy of marriage by correlating Maslow's hierarchy of needs to Christian marriage. If you step into marriage keeping score and seeking your own actualization, you have missed out on the real joy of Christian marriage. If you choose to care for your spouse regardless of if your so-called needs are being met, you are more likely to be content and fulfilled. How do you define needs? Is there anything in your relationship that is imperative? In other words, if your spouse doesn't provide this, will you walk away? Now, with the conditions or lack thereof being clear, discuss your desires and the things you would like to be present in your relationship.

"You're blessed when you get your inside world—your mind and heart—put right. Then you can see God in the outside world."[6]

All of life is spiritual. We tend to define marital problems as outside problems, but in reality they always stem from a deeper spiritual setback. Choose together to acknowledge the spiritual realities that face your emerging union and pray together that you will live your lives honestly before God and one another. If you will seek forgiveness from God and one another, accepting responsibility for your sin and selfishness, you will avoid many marital pitfalls.

"You're blessed when you can show people how to cooperate instead of compete or fight. That's when you discover who you really are, and your place in God's family."[7]

In marriage two people become one person—so when you fight, you're actually fighting yourself. Don't wear yourselves out by becoming your own worst enemies. Seek peace. What are your current patterns for dealing with conflict? Are there some things that need to change? Does anger ever get the best of you? Neither of you is perfect, and you will both fail one another, so make a choice to seek reconciliation gently and faithfully.

"You're blessed when your commitment to God provokes persecution. The persecution drives you even deeper into God's kingdom."[8]

Pastor Al Detter retold a story of his marital journey in an article for *Leadership Journal*. He said:

> *"On Valentine's Day five years earlier, I found the first Valentine's card I had ever given Marie. As I embraced her, I*

told her how grateful I was for our 25 years together, our four children, our parents who were all still living, and a ministry together that had known many blessings and few problems. What I said next seems, in retrospect, prophetic: 'But, we won't arrive at the end of the next 25 years like we have these. Almost everything will change. Our parents will die, our children will leave home, and we will face hardships like we have never known.'"

As soon as Al spoke these words, it seems his life was thrown into the toilet. With a story that could make Job himself cry, Al faced the darkness and allowed his marriage and inner life to thrive under fire. How do the two of you deal with adversity? It is not a matter of if, but when life will get hard, so prepare yourselves for love and marriage when it seems everything is against you.

"Let me tell you why you are here. You're here to be salt-seasoning that brings out the God-flavors of this earth. If you lose your saltiness, how will people taste godliness? You've lost your usefulness and will end up in the garbage." Here's another way to put it: You're here to be light, bringing out the God-colors in the world. God is not a secret to be kept. We're going public with this, as public as a city on a hill. If I make you light-bearers, you don't think I'm going to hide you under a bucket, do you? I'm putting you on a light stand. Now that I've put you there on a hilltop, on a light stand—shine! Keep open house; be generous with your lives. By opening up to others, you'll prompt people to open up with God, this generous Father in heaven."[9]

So, what are your goals and dreams for your new family? If it is anything less than the work of the Gospel and seeking the kingdom of God here on earth, then it is time to re-examine your priorities. How can your family seek justice and engage culture with the beautiful story of redemption for all people? Will your finances reflect this priority?

"Let's not pretend this is easier than it really is. If you want to live a morally pure life, here's what you have to do: You have to blind your right eye the moment you catch it in a lustful leer. You have to choose to live one-eyed or else be dumped on a moral trash pile. And you have to chop off your right hand the moment you notice it raised threateningly. Better a bloody stump than your entire being discarded for good in the dump."[10]

So, stop pretending and talk about the reality of sin in each of your lives. How can you be diligent about avoiding those traps in the future? Will you share your deepest thoughts and struggles with one another? Will you hide your dark thoughts or pretend you do not have them? If you choose to live in a truly open and honest marriage you may help one another avoid impending disasters. Remember the teaching of Christ that what is hidden will be found. Sin only grows in the dark, so bring it out into the light and deal with it together.

"Remember the Scripture that says, 'Whoever divorces his wife, let him do it legally, giving her divorce papers and her legal rights'? Too many of you are using that as a cover for selfishness and whim, pretending to be righteous just because you are 'legal.' Please, no more pretending. If you divorce your wife, you're responsible for making her an adulteress (unless she has already made herself that by sexual promiscuity). And if you marry such a divorced adulteress, you're automatically an adulterer yourself. You can't use legal cover to mask a moral failure."[11]

Does my wife need to know every thought I have and

every struggle I go through? Does honesty mean that you tell everything all the time?

What do the two of you believe about divorce? Is it ever appropriate? Share your personal and family experiences with divorce and how they form your opinion. How can you make choices to help both of you live out what you believe? For instance, is it acceptable to joke about or threaten divorce in the midst of conflict?

Dating should prepare you for the reality and intimacy of marriage. The words of Jesus penetrate our facades and allow us to see our partner in with unflinching honesty.

THERE ARE CERTAINLY SITUATIONS IN WHICH MEEKA IS DIRECTLY IMPACTED BY LINGERING THOUGHTS OR STRUGGLES AT WHICH TIMES I MUST SPEAK. THE SAME IS TRUE FOR HER. IF LINGERING THOUGHTS AND FEARS AND STRUGGLES ARE GUARDED AS SECRETS, THE RELATIONSHIP WILL SUFFER. THE LIVING RULE WOULD BE SOMETHING LIKE THE FOLLOWING: IF YOUR SPOUSE ASKS YOU DIRECTLY ABOUT A PARTICULAR THOUGHT OR STRUGGLE, THEN TOTAL HONESTY IS THE ONLY ANSWER. IT ONLY MAKES SENSE FOR ME TO NOT HOLD ANYTHING BACK FROM MEEKA IF I AM TRULY LIVING A CONFESSIONAL LIFE BEFORE GOD. FROM THAT HUMBLE POSTURE, THE WISDOM OF WHAT TO SHARE AND WHAT NOT TO SHARE WILL FLOW. —CK

Then we begin the edifying journey of becoming better people together than we are apart.

DISCUSSION QUESTIONS:

1. Have either of you bought into a certain dating philosophy, or have you "kissed dating legalism goodbye"? How would you characterize your dating experiences (together and historically), and how would you do it differently?

2. Have you sought advice about your relationship from people who know you well? Who do you trust to speak into your life? Make some immediate plans to seek those people out and invite their prayers, counsel, and criticism.

3. Are you content where you are? It is easy to miss the joy of your engaged life wishing you were already married. Commit to one another your desire to enjoy each day together and your current place in life.

4. What was it like to talk together about the struggles that may face you in the future (i.e. your parents dying)? Do you find comfort knowing you will face these challenges together?

1. Matthew 5:3 (MES)

2. Matthew 5:4 (MES)

3. Matthew 5:5 (MES)

4. Matthew 5:6 (MES)

5. Matthew 5:7 (MES)

6. Matthew 5:8 (MES)

7. Matthew 5:9 (MES)

8. Matthew 5:10 (MES)

9. Matthew 5:13-16 (MES)

10. Matthew 5:29-30 (MES)

11. Matthew 5:31-32 (MES)

"At present we are on the outside of the world, the wrong side of the door."

—C.S. Lewis[1]

2. A GENESIS VISION

The marriage debate is raging. Pastors, politicians, therapists, movie stars, and activists are weighing in with their insight. There are those who want to expand marriage's horizons beyond Judeo-Christian values. Television and movie producers are bringing same-sex unions into mainstream. Live-in partners are no longer a social oddity; couples who aren't married are openly questioning the need for a "ceremony" to substantiate their commitment. Relationship within popular culture and among its icons does appear to be subservient to a me-first value system strongly in place.

Jewish, Islamic, and Christian leaders and followers feel themselves on the defense in this changing climate. The loosening of the marriage vow threatens society and will eventually bring judgment from on high. One look at the headlines, though, and it is readily evident that healthy human relationships and marriages aren't religious people's birthright. The pedophilic priests, promiscuous pastors, and male dominant Islamic cultures show their obvious weaknesses.

Jesus of Nazareth's teaching resonates in this particular climate. "Are you tired? Worn out? Burned out on religion? Come to me. Get away with me and you'll recover your life."

Jesus is the living, breathing embodiment of God's creative and redemptive Word. The Word that spoke the world into being as depicted in the Genesis creation narrative is in bodily form in the life of Jesus. When Jesus steps into human history and begins to teach and preach, He is inviting people—then and now—into the rhythms and designs of God.

"Learn the unforced rhythms of grace. I won't lay

anything heavy or ill-fitting on you. Keep company
with me and you'll learn to live freely and lightly." Jesus
recovers in life and deed the meaning of creation as it
exists in the mind of God. Following Jesus' teaching
for marriage, then, doesn't tell you how to settle your
arguments or raise your children exactly. He isn't telling
you how to budget your money or manage your time.
Jesus is re-envisioning the essence of life, of marriage
on earth as designed by God. Jesus is rethinking the
dead-end of self-serving life and empty religion. Jesus is
leading us to read Genesis again.

"I'm holding you to the original plan ... Not everyone
is mature enough to live a married life. It requires ...
grace."

IN THE BEGINNING

> God said, "It's not good for Man to be alone; I'll make him a
> helper, a companion."
> So God formed from the dirt of the ground all the animals
> of the field and all the birds of the air ... but he didn't find a
> suitable companion. God put the Man into a deep sleep. As
> he slept he removed one of his ribs and replaced it with flesh.

God then used the rib that he had taken from the Man to make Woman and presented her to the Man.

The Man said, "Finally! Bone of my bone, flesh of my flesh! Name her Woman for she was made from Man."

Therefore a man leaves his father and mother and embraces his wife. They become one flesh.

The two of them, the Man and his Wife, were naked, but they felt not shame.[2]

Many well-meaning Christian apologists have high-jacked the creation story in Genesis. Instead of seeing the mystery and beauty within the narrative in which we are introduced to our Creator, the story is used to defend our belief in God, as though the Truth were somehow impersonal. It has been enlisted to carefully disprove evolution and force people to believe that God loves them. It's no wonder why people of faith live disconnected from and disinterested in this all-important beginning. As a result, people of faith have a weak vision for their life on earth, their relationships, and their marriages. They lack the rich context and fuel that Genesis offers for such a vision.

Our faith is rooted in the creation story. Jesus' prayer

in Matthew 6 is founded in and hoping for creation as God designed, as depicted in Genesis' early chapters. It is a celebration of what is true and what is coming true. Similarly, the Psalms confront our indifference toward God as creator with an imaginative creation faith. As one writer says of creation faith:

> Creation here is not a theory about how the world came to be. It is rather an affirmation that God's faithfulness and goodness are experienced as generosity, continuity, and regularity. Life is experienced as protected space. Chaos is not present to us and is not permitted a hearing in this well-ordered world.[3]

Just as mountains, people, snow, and cell division are part of God's creation, so is marriage. A creation faith, then, speaks of creation not as an end in itself. To speak of creation is to really speak of the Creator. It is to speak of the glory and power and kingdom of the Creator. It is to have a voice like that found in Psalm 104:30:

THIS IS VERY TRUE—WHEN YOU FINALLY ACKNOWLEDGE THAT LIFE AND MARRIAGE ARE NOT ABOUT YOUR OWN HAPPINESS, YOU ARE FREE. —CS

When you send your Spirit,
they are created,
and you renew the face of the earth.

Ultimately, God's purpose in your journey to become
one transcends simply ensuring your long, happy
life together. God is singular in His purpose in that
every aspect of your life, through the highs and lows,
through ordinary and extraordinary moments, is for the
revelation of God's glory. That is what all of creation is
singing. That is what marriage is all about. From that
place we put together a compelling vision for marriage.
In an effort to manage the mystery introduced in the
first few chapters of the Bible, the Church has boiled
down relationship to accountability partners—sin
management.[4] The fact that biblical relationship is an
expression of all that is right in the universe seemingly
makes very little difference. Answering the consumer
demand for a better life leaves little room for cultivating
this vision. We see in the creation story that human
relationship, of which marriage is the forerunner, is
necessitated by a relationship with God.

Adam is with God in Eden. It is paradise. Creator and

creation are unmediated. But man is created in God's image. And God is Trinity, relationship. Thus, that image begins to desire fulfillment. "It was not good that man should be alone." Long before sin entered the picture, relationship was on the scene. Relationship was a radiating picture of what was True in creation. Therefore, when Adam sees Eve for the first time, he breaks out in song!

More than her physical beauty, the desire for companionship, which sprung from God's presence, was fulfilled. God was glorified in Adam's fulfillment! Therefore a husband's enjoyment of his wife and a wife of her husband goes beyond simply satisfying a basic, instinctual drive for sexual gratification. Their enjoyment of each other and their oneness affirms, "God's faithfulness and goodness are experienced as generosity, continuity, and regularity."[5] God has a design. In a Christ-centered, kingdom-come marriage, a husband and wife are taking part in God's redemptive plan. "Marriage, indeed, is more than a religious metaphor: it is a first tangible and visible and most glorious fruit of the Kingdom of God."[6]

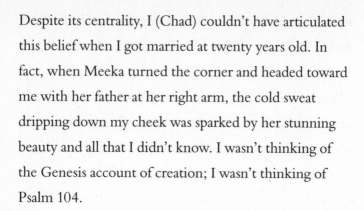
Despite its centrality, I (Chad) couldn't have articulated
this belief when I got married at twenty years old. In
fact, when Meeka turned the corner and headed toward
me with her father at her right arm, the cold sweat
dripping down my cheek was sparked by her stunning
beauty and all that I didn't know. I wasn't thinking of
the Genesis account of creation; I wasn't thinking of
Psalm 104.

My perspective has come with thirteen years of life
together. Each day our relationship moves ahead,
our hope and trust increase. The stakes have risen
dramatically. Three children, leadership in our
community of faith, and our own personal expectations
have demanded that there be a compelling vision. Our
blurry ideas and baggage from past relationships came
into sharp focus three years into our marriage. At that
juncture, again, the ability to articulate it now is much
stronger than in the moment. But we knew we needed
something more than sex and job security and plans for
children and buying a home to keep us together. Our
vision had to be deeper and more compelling than each
other. My commitment to Meeka and hers to me had
to transcend each other. I had committed my life to

something eternal as much as I had committed to being a well-behaved, faithful provider.

Meeka and I needed a vision of God's presence in and radiating through our marriage. Beyond a permanent accountability partner, we are meant to reveal God's eternal intentions for creation. Together, in other words, we reveal a very important part of God's relational existence. Too many couples have meager survival as their vision. They are fighting to stay happy and interested. The center doesn't hold.

"We are half hearted creatures, fooling around with drink and sex and ambition when infinite joy is offered us … We are far too easily pleased."[7] C.S. Lewis' commentary on Christians strikes deep. Into all our busy efforts and best intentions, Lewis speaks prophetically when he says we are "far too easily pleased." Beneath the buzz of activity, beneath all the talk of relationship in the Church, there is so little substance. Lewis goes on to say, "Our Lord finds our desires not too strong, but too weak."

Reading and meditating on the story of creation reveals

the origin of relationship and thus fuels a God-ward
vision of relationship in marriage. Our struggles and
downfalls don't necessitate relationship; sin threatens
relationship, as it does all of God's creation.

From a different perspective, the true image comes into
focus. Relationship flows from the one true God whose
essence is relational. He is three in one. Marriage's place
on earth will, according to Jesus, give way to perfect
existence in heaven. The final installment of God's
kingdom will perfectly connect God with creation and
creation with creation. Marriage is a harbinger of the
coming reality.

By returning to the Genesis narrative and allowing
that narrative to construct our vision for marriage,
our conversation moves into its larger, and more
illuminating context. In the preface of The Message,
Eugene Peterson states a critical fact about Scripture and
why we should recover a better reading of it:

"Bible reading is a means of listening to and obeying
God, not gathering religious data by which we can be
our gods. You are going to hear stories in this Book that

will take you out of your preoccupation with yourself and into the spacious freedom in which God is working the world's salvation."

When it comes to issues related to marriage and relationships, Scripture has been misused like no other aspect of our lives. Scripture is often indirect and downplays our thirst for immediate gratification. Instead of rushing toward questions of who-does-what, a newly married couple would do well to return to the biblical narrative so as to understand why we are doing what we are doing. Let's first wrestle with God's image reflected in male and female before we start dividing up jobs. In all of this and in the final analysis, Jesus' redemption frames gender (the raw material of marriage). What flows is a gracious place of sharing life and load, of give and take.

Beyond Roles

Our uniqueness in gender is an expression of God's image. We are drawing one another back to the source of our being: God. As we have said, marriage is one of God's most powerful tools whereby hearts are aligned with God's eternal purposes. Instead of simply living together and partnering for life, a husband and wife are living dangerously vulnerable and trusting, honest yet shameless, God-glorifying lives.

Through all the passion and enjoyment, even in struggles and chaos, in Christ we are confident that God's glory and not our shame or success will have the final say. Paul draws upon God's original intention:

> *Wives, understand and support your husbands in ways that show your support for Christ. The husband provides leadership to his wife the way Christ does to his church, not by domineering but by cherishing ...*

> *Husbands, go all the way in your love for your wives, exactly as Christ did for the church—a love marked by giving, not getting.*[8]

Jesus brings mercy and grace into a creation plagued by shame and sin. Instead of exalting my agenda and my needs and my desires, Paul is envisioning marriage that exalts God. God's exaltation makes the deepest possible satisfaction in marriage a reality. The husband is to live a sacrificial life as modeled by Christ. Similarly, the wife is living submissively, not subserviently. Neither of these categories make sense when our focus is on a hierarchical list of jobs and roles in marriage. Because we measure greatness in positions of power and rank, of self-promotion and personal achievement, submission has often been equated to a less-than-glamorous job. In kingdom-of-God reality, however, a man and woman's greatness arises from his or her service to God for others.

A husband and wife are, instead, living first and foremost before God. Our ultimate submission is to God's plan and to God's kingdom. The husband's sacrifice has very real implications for his wife and his children; it is intended for and in response to God's mercy. A wife's submission, while impacting her husband and children, is an offering unto God. God is looking even if others aren't. The greatest in God's kingdom is Jesus Christ. Jesus reminded the disciples of this truth:

> It's not going to be that way with you. Whoever wants to be great must become a servant. Whoever wants to be first among you must be your slave. That is what the Son of Man has done: He came to serve, not be served.[9]

Back to Genesis. "Helper" is a weak translation of the Hebrew word "ezer" in Genesis. Peterson approaches a more accurate translation in The Message by adding, "companion." To be sure, God intends far more for the woman than administrating her husband's plan. By looking at where "ezer" is used elsewhere in the Old Testament, we begin to get a more accurate picture of the importance of relationship between husband and wife:

> *Hear, O Lord, the cry of Judah;*
> *bring him to his people.*
> *With his own hands he defends his cause.*
> *Oh, be his help against his foes!*[10]

Or, elsewhere,

> *May he send you help from the sanctuary*
> *and grant you support from Zion.*[11]

Also, read Solomon's poem in Proverbs 31. Unfortunately, this poem is treated as unrealistic or belittling, as if it were a job description to be carefully followed. Instead, Solomon, similar to the Psalmists, is celebrating what he sees as God's beautiful, albeit subtle and oft overlooked creation on display in female. Solomon's attention is rapt, soaking in the beauty and calling attention to the wife of noble character; she is living ezer glory.

Like Jesus calling attention to the subtle and overlooked beauty of the birds of the air and lilies of the field, Solomon is drawing our attention to the reality of God's image in the woman. The wife of noble character is living a strong, self-giving, creative, shrewd, and submissive life all at once. By submitting to God's glorious intention, she is able to give herself to her family and community without fear and anxiety of meaningless, lowly existence. Her meaning and purpose are in God. Shame is nowhere to be found!

If what we seek is God's vision of marriage versus self-enhancement in marriage, shame is less likely to take root. The garden, though, must be cultivated and tended by both husband and wife. Just as God's plan is thwarted by obvious self-seeking motivation, so it is with subtle and secret self-contempt. This is especially true for men. The domineering and deadly discord that threatens so many marriages, especially dangerous for the wife and children, stems from a fearful and cowardly man.

For too long the feminist agenda and what I will label the fundamental-traditionalist agenda have collided, resulting in very little change. Feminist and professor Elizabeth Fox-Genovese said of these two extremes, "Conservatives talk as if they want to imprison women in motherhood; feminists talk as if they want to liberate women from it." Her conclusion leads her to a new way of thinking she calls "family feminism."[12]

The feminists were partially right in that women have been exploited and abused by a domineering society. The extent of the damage and the blanketed responsibility placed upon all men is often confused in this

EVENTUALLY A STRONG EMPHASIS ON FULFILLING ROLES MAKES ONE FEEL LIKE AN OBJECT RATHER THAN A PERSON, LIKE BEING "APPRECIATED" ONLY FOR WHAT YOU DO INSTEAD OF CELEBRATED FOR WHO YOU ARE! —LS

movement. The fundamentalists were partially right in pointing toward God, and yet they stopped way short by using Scripture as a means to their chauvinistic ends. Both missed the relationship as redeemed in Christ.

Many well meaning couples early in their marriages silently agree to roles that undermine the integrity of the relationship. Initially, these roles seem to fit together nicely, compensating for each other's weaknesses or inhibitions. Over time, however, it becomes painfully clear that the agreement is fraught with error. In my work with couples, I call this destructive or negative compatibility. As it matures and strengthens its hold on a marriage it leads to hopeless resignation.

Once God's vision is off the radar, each other's weaknesses land center stage, creating a cycle of destruction.

CHAD AND I WORK HARD AT WORKING TOGETHER IN EVERY AREA OF OUR HOME. WE CAN'T AFFORD TO ABANDON EACH OTHER IN ANY AREA OF OUR RELATIONSHIP. —MEEKA KARGER

Psychologist and developmental theorist Carol Gilligan has described this reality in her landmark study. The results were published and discussed in detail in her book *In a Different Voice*. Gilligan documents an error that is as common in marriage as it is subtle.

The false assumption for men is that if they know themselves well enough, they will know others, namely their wives. Thus men, despite the popular myths put forth about men lacking the ability for introspection, spend exorbitant time imprisoned in their own thoughts and ideas. For this reason, fantasy (especially sexual) is an area of struggle for many men. It is not uncommon to find men living totally disconnected lives, marooned in a world of their own making. Not only are they living un-sacrificially, they haven't a clue how to begin serving their wives and children beyond making monthly deposits at the bank.

Women, on the other hand, err by assuming that they will know themselves to the extent that they know others. If men live fundamentally disconnected lives, women live dissociated from themselves, a disconnection from God working around and within them. Women grow to resent the constant demands made on them by family members. With each demand, their identity is being further subdivided. Into this maelstrom, submission feels like a death sentence. Leaving seems like the only alternative to dying.

As poignant as Gilligan's observations are, the thrust of her conclusion misses the point. Instead of the way out of this prison cell being the recovery of the woman's voice in relationship (though that is definitely part of it), freedom, again, will come as we place our minds on God's design as laid out (sometimes indirectly, subtly) in Scripture, while we confess our absolute need for Christ's redemption.

Thoughtless movement toward and fixation on "roles" in a marriage breeds selfishness and insecurities. Instead of healthy boundaries, the relationship grows lifeless. The premature search for roles persists because of the insecurity all of us feel in marriage. Grabbing at roles is like grabbing gods—roles are security. Roles become secret handshakes between husbands and wives that allow each other to live in autopilot, as it were, without improvisation, insecurity, or relationship. Jesus calls us to seek God's kingdom and God's righteousness as we travel through the unknown.

My identity as a husband is rooted in God, not in jobs I do or don't do. A healthy and growing relationship will involve people who are operating outside of conventional jobs or roles. The tension that exists between the excesses of traditional fundamentalists and liberal, progressives should be seen as a creative tension instead of a destructive one. A healthy marriage lives in that tension, caving into neither excess.

The "handshake" gives me a chill. I have visions of a husband routinely kicked back in his chair every evening, remote in hand, sports on TV. While he escapes the "pressures" of his work, hers are never-ending. She's left alone to suffer in silence.

A couple willing to live and build a life together within this tension will create an environment in which each member of the family selflessly contributes to the overall functioning in the home. An attitude like that of Christ's forms the living, beating heart of a home. It is the cornerstone of a marriage. There will be a selfless servant's attitude permeating every corner of the house. Couples, thus, set the tone their children follow. Kids will have grown up seeing their dads help out in the carpool and in the kitchen and leading the family through complex decision-making. They will know their mom to be a shrewd manager within the home, providing insight into financial decisions and exploring her own hobbies, as well as seeing to endless mounds of laundry.

The glory of God will be radiating from within such a home. Others will see the people giving and taking, jobs performed, and roles assumed. Upon closer inspection, though, they will see hearts devoted to the well-being of others and fidelity to a calling much larger than family life or happy marriage. They will experience a passion for the purposes and design of God. The passionate pursuit, as we will see in the next chapter, takes a couple through unromantic but no less intimate territories. It is a sacred journey.

DISCUSSION QUESTIONS:

1. Read the creation story together and separate, out loud. Look for subtleties and nuances that in the past you have overlooked. Journal and think through the following questions:

- What images are especially vivid to you in the narrative?
- What is God doing according to the text?
- Read Psalms 104 as further thought and images of God and creation.
- Consider the fact that Adam is incomplete even before

sin enters the story. How does Adam come to experience this lack? What is his response to Eve?

2. How does the discussion about roles and the idea that we run after roles at the expense of relationship change or challenge your thinking? Consider Lisa's and Meeka's perspective as noted in their sidebars. How can couples find liberation in this area as opposed to imprisonment?

3. How does Christ's attitude as described in Philippians 2 fuel your discussion and motivation?

4. In your family growing up, would you say that the roles assumed by Mom and Dad were traditional or liberal? Was it common to see you parents sharing roles or strictly adhering to set jobs?

5. In what ways have you seen Carol Gilligan's description of relationship error play out in your present and past relationships? The error is as follows: Men believe that if they know themselves, they will know and connect with others. Women believe that if they know others, they will know and connect with themselves.

6. All of us have tried to suppress our deepest desires—sexually and emotionally—but real faith is about re-embracing these desires. Discuss this truth with your partner. Share with your partner what you desire for marriage.

1. C.S. Lewis, *The Weight of Glory and Other Addresses* (New York: Touchstone, 1996), 37.

2. Genesis 2:18-25 (MES)

3. Walter Brueggemann, *The Message of the Psalms: A Theological Commentary*, (Augsburg: Minneapolis, 1984), 26.

4. For more on the fallacy of sin management ailing so much of the Church today, see Dallas Willard, *The Divine Conspiracy*, (Harper: San Francisco, 1998).

5. Brueggemann, *Message of the Psalms*, 26.

6. Mike Mason, *The Mystery of Marriage: As Iron Sharpens Iron*, (Multnomah: Portland, 1985), 24.

7. Lewis, *Weight of Glory*, 26.

8. Ephesians 5:22-24 (MES)

9. Mark 10:43-45 (MES)

10. Deuteronomy 33:7

11. Psalm 20:2

12. As quoted by Jennifer C. Braceras in her article "June Cleaver Wants Flex Time," appearing in *Independent Women's Forum*, Spring 2003.

"We're the insect life of paradise:
Crawl across leaf
Or among towering blades of grass
Glimpse only sometimes
the amazing breadth of heaven."
—Bruce Cockburn[1]

3. AN UNROMANTIC JOURNEY

Unless a couple finds beauty and pleasure in the simple, ordinary places in their life together, marriage's initial excitement will soon fade into unbearable boredom. This truth reminds me of a particular birthday gift I gave to Meeka and her friends' reaction to the gift. We had been married about three years.

We had just moved from Houston to Denver. We were making some changes in our wardrobe as fall changed to winter. Meeka, having grown up in Calgary, Alberta, knew how to keep it real and practical, while remaining beautiful and warm. When I would go visit her during the chilly Canadian winter months, she wore these white flannel pajamas that were simple but sexy nevertheless. She looked great in them. I loved that she liked flannel!

Having left the pajamas in Canada when we got married three years earlier, I knew exactly what I was going to get her now that we were in Denver. When she revealed to her girlfriends at the office that I had given her new flannel pajamas, they were floored! They wondered how I could be so utterly out of touch with what is really sexy. Didn't I know what a woman wanted?

"Flannel isn't sexy. Silk is sexy," they reminded Meeka. But Meeka likes flannel, and if Meeka likes flannel, I like flannel. In fact, I like any fabric—cotton, silk, or burlap—that hangs from her beautiful body!

Consider Jesus' timeless teaching on simplicity and perspective. "Don't hoard treasure down here where it gets eaten by moths and corroded by rust or—worse!—stolen by burglars. Stockpile treasure in heaven, where it is safe from moth and rust and burglars. It's obvious, isn't it? The place where your treasure is, is the place you will most want to be, and end up being."

Once we commit our hearts to see beauty as dictated by conventional wisdom, popular forms, or what money can buy, we have lowered ourselves. We have dulled our vision and numbed our heart's desires. Jesus, on the other hand, is inviting us to strive for a deeper albeit subtle standard of beauty and enjoyment in life and marriage. While costly, romance as God has designed it is life-giving and connected to the heart of a person. It has less to do with what is easily seen and self-enhanced and more to do with Him.

We Are Withdrawn

While sacred, the journey to become one is by and large unromantic. It's not so much that the romance disappears. The relationship matures, and romance takes on a less obvious form. The radar for romance developed during courtship must be fine-tuned for the rugged countryside of marriage. Along the way, the eyes and ears of our heart must be cultivated to find beauty hidden among the ordinary, less spectacular crags. The ability to see and hear is no less than a spiritual sense that must be cultivated.

Thomas Merton has said of such a perspective, "One of

the most important—and most neglected—elements in the beginnings of the interior life is the ability to respond to reality, to see value and beauty in ordinary things, to come alive to the splendor that is all around us in the creatures of God. We do not see these things because we have withdrawn from them." This truth when applied to marriage is life changing. We live lives obsessed with "the new," seeking after the latest technology, breaking news, and temporal thrills. Marriage is an unfathomable well that calls us continually to a deeper place. That space does not allow for the pleasantries of the new and the shallow. So we must re-enter the deeper space in our own lives, and from that space, we begin to share and commune together.

Reentry is painful and difficult. Anyone can appreciate the rush of a first kiss, but what will a kiss be like when the kids are screaming their heads off, the house is a mess, and his breath is lethal? Gone is the Hollywood formula for romance or the knee-knocking wiles of youthful infatuation. In its place, however, is romance that is deeper and wider, reflecting a sacred covenant between God and humanity. Years of indifference toward cultivating an "interior life" dull our spiritual

perception and sensitivity to God's subtle and hidden
work. Author and naturalist Annie Dillard said that
reentry will come as we "cultivate a healthy poverty and
simplicity" in areas of our life. She continued, "What
you see is what you get."

Truth is, many couples are staring into the bright lights
lining a destructive path. They don't want to think
about the fading infatuation, the sagging boobs, and
diminished sex-drive around the corner. Like thousands
of marriages dying today, poor choices are to blame
for the blind and deaf hearts within those marriages.
A devotional life of cultivating a hunger only God can
satisfy takes hard work and deliberate effort. A couple
must be working at this even when the other isn't
looking. Jesus taught that we should find a "closet,"
go there, and experience the invisible God's gaze. The
relief of finally finding and marrying the "right person"
often opens the door to a complacency that abandons a
life of real and utter dependence on God early on in the
marriage.

The "healthy poverty" of which Dillard spoke looks
like a simple and honest and curious life. (She's not

promoting problem-free living.) Such a life leads toward deeper faith and is the result of faith. It is welcome relief from the relentless pace most couples find themselves living (especially when children enter the picture). The narrow path that leads to life Jesus spoke of seems awkward and indirect compared to the brightly lit path of destruction.

Thousands of Smaller Steps

After a recent soccer practice, my oldest son, Reece, told me he wanted to play World Cup soccer. Wanting to encourage such dreams while also helping him to see at an early age the requirements of such a goal, I (Chad) asked him a question. "How many steps are there on the field between the two goals?"

He thought for a moment, mumbled as though he were counting in his head, and said, "Fifteen!" Again, trying to balance dreams and reality, I told him I thought that there were probably a few more than fifteen but that he had made good guess. "In other words," I began, "you can't get to the other end of the field in one step. There are many, many small steps between the goals."

"In the same way," I went on to tell him, "between this moment in your soccer life and a World Cup moment are thousands of smaller steps. Today's practice was one of those steps, Reece."

Similarly, life on the narrow path must be approached deliberately and with discipline. It will cost us a great deal. Entering haphazardly will only lead to lots of hazard. The hand of your spouse should be a strong and steady reminder. A day at a time is sustainable. Seeing the other as your ally is imperative.

Seek First

Indulgence and consumerism that is embedded in most couples' lives after twenty-five years of marriage chokes the vision that once burned singularly in their hearts. They perhaps feel as though a thief robbed their joy in the middle of the night. In reality, however, the ebb and flow of life matched with their indifference toward cultivating a Christ-centered life paved the way

HUSBANDS, IT IS OF EXTREME IMPORTANCE THAT YOU ARE ACTIVELY PURSUING GOD. THAT CREATES A SECURITY FOR YOUR WIFE, ENABLING HER TO TRUST YOU MORE AND ENCOURAGE HER IN HER OWN FAITH JOURNEY. DO NOT BE LAZY ABOUT THIS!
—MK

to the place they have arrived. This predicament didn't arrive overnight; the way out will take time.

The demand of what we thought was really important has a way of silencing the "still small voice of God" hidden in the ordinary corners of each individual life; once the two individuals are indifferent toward the voice of God in their hearts, their vision for the relationship begins to cool. This brings on a wave of panic and unfamiliarity. "How did we arrive here? I don't feel like I love her anymore." It's at this point that Jesus' call to seek first the kingdom of God and the righteousness of God seems so counterintuitive. What feels most natural is to work on the marriage! Nothing could be further from the truth.

IF YOU BUY INTO THE "MEET MY NEEDS" VERSION OF CHRISTIAN MARRIAGE COMMON IN BOOKS LIKE *HIS NEEDS, HER NEEDS*, YOU WILL SPEND YOUR LIFE CHASING ALL THE WRONG THINGS—SELF-ACTUALIZATION IS NOT YOUR GOAL. —CS

When your relationship grows complicated, sagging beneath disappointments and boredom, it feels quite natural to seek first satisfaction, excitement, or romance. Plenty of talk these days leads us to try harder, appear sexier, and read more about a Christian marriage.

Contrary to all of the noise, Jesus draws our attention
to the most unlikely place: "Look at the birds of the air;
they do not sow or reap or store away in barns, and yet
your heavenly Father feeds them ... See how the lilies of
the field grow." While Jesus is emphasizing the basics of
life like food, water, and shelter, I think it safe to say that
most of our worries in life are challenged in Matthew 6.
At the close of this chapter, Jesus highlights the thrust of
all He has said up till now, "Seek first his kingdom and
his righteousness, and all these things will be given to
you as well."

It is unfortunate that many well-meaning pastors have
taken precious time to
preach, "Seek first a
healthy and balanced
marriage." In an effort to be relevant to their audience,
pastors succumb to the same trap we mentioned above
about worry. Make the earthly thing you are worried
about the center of your focus, and if you look hard
enough and follow these seven steps, you will have a
healthy marriage.

IF YOU GET NOTHING ELSE IN
THIS BOOK, GET THIS "SEEK FIRST"
PART! —LS

By looking at something other than yourself, Jesus says, you begin to see something very important. It's as if Jesus is saying, "I'm doing something far greater than making a way for Christian marriage." The point of looking at the lilies and the birds was to remind you of this greater work: Absolute dependency upon God for God's glory in your life and marriage. Insofar as we refuse to follow Jesus' teaching on this matter, a so-called good Christian marriage, ironically, becomes one more form of idolatry, and the cycle begins again.

As it applies to marriage, Jesus is getting at basic truth in Matthew 6. You were made for more than a happy Christian marriage. Marriage takes its proper place as yet another vehicle through which God's glory is seen and experienced. You, and thus your marriage, like the lilies and the birds, are absolutely dependent upon the living, creating, sustaining God of the universe. Simplicity leads a person to this and grows out of this "seek first God" focus. Marriage becomes a profound reflection of God's agenda. Every moment, then, good or bad, is dependent upon God. Picking up Jesus' teaching in Matthew 7, we find practical guides for a couple to become promoters of God's glorious design.

Nature

"Instead of looking at the fashions, walk out into the fields and look at the wildflowers ... If God gives such attention to the appearance of wildflowers—most of which are never ever seen—don't you think he'll attend to you?"

Going outside, spending time in nature puts us into our proper place. Gone are the layers of protection that insulate us from unpredictable elements. We begin to find our place among the other creations of God, but we also begin to grow more interdependent upon that creation and, most importantly, the Creator. This is precisely what Jesus is inviting us into.

As Merton says in the quote at the outset of this chapter, we have withdrawn from this sort of life. We've, in other words, gone and remained locked up inside. Look at the flowers and birds. Take Jesus at His Word. Go outside. Take a closer look at the balance in creation of interdependence and sustainability.

GET RID OF DISTRACTIONS FOR A WHILE. GO FOR A WALK. —MK

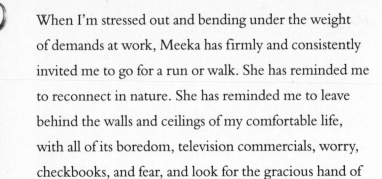

When I'm stressed out and bending under the weight of demands at work, Meeka has firmly and consistently invited me to go for a run or walk. She has reminded me to reconnect in nature. She has reminded me to leave behind the walls and ceilings of my comfortable life, with all of its boredom, television commercials, worry, checkbooks, and fear, and look for the gracious hand of God together.

Our boredom and worry have more to do with our spiritual indifference and immobilization than they do with God's absence or silence. We don't need more idle entertainment! Make plans for your time alone in nature and time together in nature. It may be a good idea to use this time for exercise, painting, or cycling!

Giving

If a couple develops a pattern of hoarding and clinging to financial security early on, then they are headed for a stingy, insecure life. Selfishness is a weak and fragile life. It will undermine a relationship. Strength and security comes from sharing. Seeing all resources as God's resources, a husband and wife's eyes are opened to the needs of others.

Many a couple has said, "Later in life when we have more money, we will give," and often the years bring increased financial resources to their family. But their giving patterns remain the same. A wild and unscientific guess is that the majority of American families spend 99 percent of their income on themselves. Scripture calls us to bring that ratio at least below 90 percent. Far from a burden, a giving life is freeing.

Start early in making plans to share with others. Plan to live as simply as you can so that you are able to respond in this way to others. Survey all of your resources and consider which of those you will give to another expecting nothing in return. Serve in the mission field or in a local community service project together. Give regularly to missions over and above your offering to the local church you attend.

Simplicity

In the car ride home the other day, I was riveted to an interview with Sting. The NPR staff noted that his latest release had as its focus the struggles and predicaments common to a Western, middle age, modest people. He agreed that that had been his intention. She then

followed her observation with a penetrating question.
She wanted to know how he, Sting, could sing about
such a life when he lived in a medieval castle, owned a
private jet, and performed concerts before thousands
of people every year. Moreover, how could you, she
wondered, be both an activist for the rain forests
and similar causes while working in marketing and
advertisement with corporate giants? He told her that he
planted one hundred something trees on his estate (near
the air conditioned castle I'm sure!). There was a day in
his life as an artist and poet that the interviewer wouldn't
have been able to ask him such challenging questions.
He probably knew simpler days.

Unfortunately, many self-proclaimed Christians give
very little real, practical consideration to Jesus' teachings.
They are trying to chase after the American Dream
on the one hand, while at the same time nodding in
agreement with Jesus' warning to refuse the amassing
of earthly treasures. All the while, they can't figure out
why they are so unhappy in their Christian marriages,
listening to their Christian music, running their
Christian businesses.

As you contemplate what simplicity may mean for you, consider a few suggested guidelines that may get you thinking in a helpful direction:

- Think before you buy; analyze your motives for making a purchase.
- Seek opportunities to give and receive nothing in return. Instead of involving yourself or your family in another social activity, consider volunteering in the community. Kids need to grow up with a model of charity, and you can help keep a women's shelter or a food bank going by helping out in addition to any financial contribution you might make. You can help with the books, write a grant, answer a phone, paint a wall, or help customers in a thrift store. All those tasks are important. Chances are they'll find things that the kids can do too.
- Adopt giving as a lifestyle; it may breathe renewed hope into a world filled with the extremely rich and the extremely poor. Dr. Charles Birch once said, "The rich must live more simply that the poor may simply live."
- Set (and keep) a monthly budget. Overspending is often a result of under planning.

- Enjoy what is free: town concerts, lectures at local universities, parks and nature preserves; the list is endless if you pay attention.

- Spend real time with your family. Read, talk, and cook dinner together. Don't substitute busyness (going to a movie, a mall, or out to dinner) for real contact. Play with your kids. Rake the lawn together. Remember that your work, your status in the community, everything the world may count as important pales in importance next to these people God has placed in your life. No one will remember ten years from now that you stayed late to finish off an account. But someone may remember that you came home early to play touch football.

Prayer

Prayer and fasting are absolutely necessary in a disciplined pursuit of God. Through prayer and fasting, we challenge the natural tendency to trust in anything or anyone else but God, which follows Jesus' teaching on sharing. A self-centered and full life is a fragile life. It becomes small and constricting, which brings on feelings of being smothered and bored.

Teacher and author Dallas Willard said this about prayer, "We can train ourselves to invoke God's presence in every action we perform." A life of prayer must be worked at and maintained. But a life of prayer is a far cry from what comes to the minds of most Westerners, Christians included. The Orthodox Church, rooted in Eastern philosophy and thought, considers prayer something deeper and more essential. "Prayer is a living relationship between persons," Bishop Kallistos Ware wrote.[2] That said, a life of prayer will come at great cost to the faithful disciple who chooses to facilitate this aspect of his life. It will be costly to the married couple that is busy, distracted, and working hard at being a good Christian couple.

A husband and a wife should incorporate prayer and fasting into their individual as well as shared life. The couple that seeks to live a prayerful life will find their awareness of others and God's work in others will be heightened. Similarly, fasting cultivates a healthy poverty. Communicate with each other regularly during these times. Keep each other posted on what God is revealing to you.

Treasures

To seek God first is to hold God—to know in my gut that God knows me—as the single most important treasure in our life. Jesus' instruction was that our real values are where our hearts are connected. He warned of making too many lasting and binding connections in this world's riches.

How do we know if our treasure is in what this world is selling? What do you buy? What do you worry about buying or affording? What do you own? What pushes the anxiety button for you most often? There,

THOUGH CHAD AND I HAVEN'T SPENT HOURS AND HOURS ON OUR KNEES TOGETHER, WE ARE DEEPLY CONNECTED, AND OUR OPEN, HONEST COMMUNICATION LEADS TO ONGOING PRAYER FOR EACH OTHER. HE KNOWS MY NEEDS AND STRUGGLES AS I KNOW HIS. —MK

in those assumed and familiar places, is where you have deposited you heart. Those are the real challenges to God's place in your life.

Trusting anything but God for life, for security, for strength will lead to profound disappointment. The challenges and demands that lie ahead for every couple will be faced with real strength and security if their treasure is God. "So to whom," Isaiah asks the ancient Hebrews, "will you compare me, the Incomparable?"

Good stuff can be empty as treasures. Nothing can compare to God. Early in a relationship, a couple will agree to value, usually with little to no verbal communication, many different things and thereby deposit their heart. The toll to the people and the marriage is costly. Often the darkness and chaos that seemingly arrives overnight is indicative of two people who are no longer searching for the Incomparable God.

Obedience vs. Knowledge

Throughout His ministry, Jesus skillfully told stories of common, everyday occurrences. He utilized ordinary life as a vivid picture of dependency upon God. He also told parables to overturn conventional wisdom about relationships and knowing God. He was a master at capturing images that point to eternal truths.

As a married person, don't make the mistake of making Jesus' subtle and powerful teaching answer your questions. Instead, allow Jesus to shape the questions you are asking. Allow the deeper truths that touch every facet of a person's life with God's eternal rhythm touch your marriage. If it was true when you were single, it is true when you are married. If it is true when you are young, it is true when you are old. Today, tomorrow, and forever, God's truth stands. A husband and wife can take Jesus at His word and follow His teachings. He is touching the heart of the matter. Our living response is our only response.

The two builders in Matthew 7 knew what was required for a strong foundation. They were both building homes with this knowledge. One, however, had other values that didn't allow him to practically value a proper foundation. He piled the sand high, hoping for the best as he saved money. The other took the harder path initially, but the one that proved secure. He chiseled the stone for a timeless foundation.

This story reveals a very important truth. Wisdom and foolishness aren't separated by ignorance. Obedience separates the two. We must take Jesus' teaching seriously. Too often He is forced to address areas He is not addressing, or His teachings are over-spiritualized. Both strip the simple lessons of Jesus of their real power.

His wisdom is by its very nature practical. It begs to be incorporated into our ordinary decisions.

The simplicity and endurance and real romance of weathering life's valleys and struggles as one is possible to the degree that you seek God first and foremost.

Patterns for Life

The rugged and unromantic terrain of "till death do us part" can be traversed if our purpose is the glory of God. The days, months, or years before children arrive are filled with opportunity to form this pattern in the relationship. Once the kids arrive, the patterns of early life together come to bear. The tyranny of the urgent threatens to co-opt a couple from what is central: Seek first ... do not worry about tomorrow.

Again, make the words of Jesus a reality in the journey of your marriage:

Ask and it will be given to you; seek and you will find; knock and the door will be opened to you. For everyone who asks receives; he who seeks finds; and to him who knocks, the door will be opened.

As disciples of Jesus Christ, your heart is courageous and tenacious. You are full of hope. God holds the combination to your heart whether through treacherous or boring or uneventful terrain. Strive to live a sacred life, not a romantic or happy life. In the chapter that follows, we explore in more detail what a sacred life unto God looks like in a marriage.

DISCUSSION QUESTIONS:

1. "Beauty is in the eye of the beholder." Get to know the beholder surveying your beauty. What has shaped his or her eyes? What is his or her heart committed to, and how does it influence their relationship with you? Read Matthew 6:19-34 in The Message.

2. "Your eyes are windows into your body. If you open your eyes wide in wonder and belief, your body fills up with light. If you live squinty-eyed in greed and distrust, your body is a dank cellar. If you pull the blinds on your windows, what a dark life you will have." Jesus' words here ought to fuel much thought and meditation as they relate to your marriage. What have the windows of your soul been subjected to as you start out in your marriage?

3. What does "seek first" God in your marriage versus your own fleeting, felt needs look like? How will you go about living God-centered lives in a marriage?

4. In what ways have you "withdrawn" from the sacredness of ordinary and simple living, as Thomas Merton stated at the beginning of the chapter?

5. Consider the different areas we cover in this chapter, as they will help you reenter the rhythm and beauty of God's creation:

- Exploring and spending time in nature. How many of your dates take place indoors? Being outside fosters conversation and shared-simplicity.
- Other than the church you attend, what else will you contribute financially to?
- What will keep your life simple so that you can give of your resources? What parts of the list we have included are challenging, new, or things you are already doing?
- Remember prayer is more about being seen by the invisible God than it is speaking to God with your spouse. Do you go into the closet on a regular basis?

Does your spouse know what struggles you are facing
or what gratitude fills your heart? Do you include
fasting as a way of letting go of the worthless treasures
on this earth?

- Good things can be bad treasures. What is distracting
  you from the "seek first God" teaching of Jesus in
  Matthew 6?

6. What will be your "little steps," disciplined and consistent,
toward living a seek first life? There's more than fifteen steps
to the other goal on the soccer field!

7. Read Jesus' entire Sermon in Matthew 5 through 7 out
loud with your spouse.

1. Cockburn, Bruce, "Isn't That What Friends Are For" (Golden Mountain Music: 1999) from the
album *Breakfast in New Orleans, Dinner in Timbuktu* (Rykodisc, 1999).

2. Ware, Bishop Kallistos, *The Orthodox Way* (Revised Edition), (St.Vladamir's Seminary Press:
New York, 1999) p. 104.

"I remember the devotion
of your youth,
How as a bride you loved me
and followed me through the desert,
through lands not sown."
—Jeremiah 2:2

4. AS UNTO GOD

The devil said it best: "Vanity: It's definitely my favorite sin."[1] No doubt, the roller coaster of life and marriage is fueled by the mistakes of "self love, the natural opiate."[2] Unchecked, we live much of our life seeking our own pleasure and gain, which begs the obvious question when it comes to marriage. A God-centered marriage goes against everything that seems natural. Why bother? Furthermore, how do we trust when a partner is consumed with selfishness? How do we give ourselves away?

Equally damaging, though less obvious at first, is finding

yourself fifteen years into a marriage vow with someone
struggling with mountains of shame and self-contempt.
By comparison, shame is more subtle, whereas vanity
is easily spotted. Both vanity and shame, though, erode
a solid foundation in marriage. Both subvert a vision of
selflessness, sacrifice, and ultimately, hope in God.

The submission called for in a biblical marriage is
mistaken, mostly for women, as a disappearing act in
which the women is seen but not heard. As we have said
in earlier chapters, simply doing your "job" in marriage
is shortsighted. Certain jobs will, no doubt, appear more
important. Submission and sacrifice turn quickly into
demeaning and belittling ideas.

Instead of the freedom and honesty meant for a husband
and wife, shame and vanity threaten the fabric of the
relationship. Insecurities and doubt will subtly and
forcefully derail a marriage. Courage and tenacity
is needed, neither of which will grow where vanity
and shame are present. In this chapter we explore the
liberation and abundance believers in Christ, both
men and women, have that makes self-denial an act of
worship instead of emotional suicide.

A Day on Sawtooth

During the two years we lived in Denver, Meeka and I (Chad) did as much hiking as we could. Not only did we love being outdoors together (and still do), it was one of the many hobbies we could afford! In particular, we loved to scale the peaks soaring above 14,000 feet. A cheap paperback we had purchased detailed the different approaches to each peak, along with the degree of difficulty of each potential route. Many of these summits were attainable in the course of a daylong hike.

One morning we headed for a relatively easy hike. We parked, got out our packs, along with our trusty fourteener book, and scaled Beirstadt in no time. As was often the case, especially for the summits close to the metropolitan Denver area, the top of the mountain was crowded. People were everywhere. This was always somewhat disconcerting. It was a beautiful day, though; the view was brilliant. Rugged peaks with frozen glaciers on their North faces seemed to touch the sky. While we ate our lunch and took all this in, I noticed a saddle connecting to another ridge leading to another peak. I found the detail of the route in my book.

Given that it was early on a beautiful a day, along
with the fact that the book described the traverse as
relatively easy, I decided we should hike Sawtooth
Ridge after lunch. The spine of the ridge was flanked
on its northwest side with a cliff that fell dramatically,
maybe five hundred feet. Meeka followed me onto this
tight, wire-like ridge a short distance before deciding to
descend down it southeast side, which was talus—the
accumulation of one or more rockslides over the years.
In addition to the sharp rocks and boulders, the slope
was steep by most standards. We descended nearly
halfway before we began to realize that we needed to
scramble back to the ridge's edge.

By now, Meeka had taken a fall and scraped her leg,
the hour was getting late, and the climb back to the
top of the ridge seemed ominous to our worrisome,
fatigued beings. We were tired, worried, and alone. No
one else was in sight. The crowds we had shunned on
Beirstadt would have been a welcomed reunion now.
I was secretly wondering how we were going to scale
this slope and, moreover, how long after dark we would
arrive back to our car. I was growing more anxious with
every step. I tried hiding my anxiety. Meeka was less

quiet about her misgivings. She followed nonetheless.
Finally, I turned to tell her we had to scramble on hands
and feet back to the top of the ridge. She looked at me
in disbelief, as if she couldn't believe she had allowed
herself to be talked into this journey. I asked her, "Don't
you trust me?"

Without a moment's hesitation, Meeka immediately
shot back, "No! I don't trust you! But I don't have a
choice." I was stunned. In that moment I knew why
I loved her and why we would struggle in the years to
come, indeed why we had struggled up until now. Her
honesty was beautiful and dangerous. I silently turned
and began to scramble over the boulders. She quietly
followed.

We reached the top, traversed the edge of the ridge, and found our car before dark. All the way back, though, I was haunted by the precision of her

THIS STORY REMINDS ME OF THE FACT THAT WE WERE MARRIED YOUNG AND ESSENTIALLY DIDN'T HAVE A CLUE WHAT LAY AHEAD. IT HAS ALWAYS BEEN CRITICAL THAT CHAD BE TRUSTWORTHY AND THAT I SHOW MYSELF TRUST-WORTHY TO HIM AS WE FACE THE UNKNOWN. BECAUSE OF THIS, TIMES OF "ADVENTURE" HAVE CERTAINLY FORGED INTIMACY.
—MK

words. She had put herself in a dubious place of trusting

someone, it seemed, who wasn't always fully deserving of her trust. She set aside her feelings, her natural inclinations, and her inhibitions and followed me across that ridge.

That day in the mountains is a vivid picture of two people sharing life in marriage. In August three years prior, Meeka had promised the rest of her natural life to me, and I promised all of myself in return. Young and clueless, we were committing to terrain, as it were, that neither of us knew (rationally and practically) how to tackle. That is precisely the power of the marriage vow. Though spoken confidently, the vow is recited with precious little assurance of what the future holds. Like Meeka agreeing to follow me that day onto Sawtooth Ridge, many a bride and groom grab each other's hands with little more than a burning desire to be together.

What will sustain the relationship when the years have resulted in hurt, loss, and sheer boredom?

Unknown to Meeka that day, her candid reply offers us some insight into the answer to that question. In the four years I had known Meeka up until that day, a greater force than our relationship was at work in her (as well as in me). God had taken ahold of her heart and begun to reshape and re-center everything around His purposes. Though self-sufficient, strong, and smart, Meeka had, along with her dependency upon God, managed to arrive at a place of self-denial without self-hatred. God was redeeming a heart that was fully His with a capacity for honest and trusting relationship with others, especially her husband. That same candid voice, sharp mind, and inner strength that I had been attracted to four years earlier hadn't disappeared. Instead, God had drawn her to love and worship Himself above all else.

A Vista of Mercy

Our two years in Denver, ironically, turned out to be two of the toughest years for us. (I say ironically because we had moved there like kids heading to the playground for extended recess!) Like that afternoon on the mountain, we had arrived at a place in our relationship where we were looking at each other stunned, angry, in love, and asking whether or not we would continue in the same way we had for three years. We had looked at each other and said essentially what Meeka had said to me, "No! I don't like you, nor do I always trust you. But

I don't have any choice." In a sense, we were praying, "God, help us. I don't necessarily like this person all the time. I will trust in You, God, as I sacrifice my self-interests and desires." God was faithful. In those two years, God provided us with a view of our lives bathed in the mercy of Jesus Christ.

Only God has the right to call for our lives since it was God who gave us our lives in the first place. God is the only one who can evoke a life of sacrifice and other-centeredness without it turning to shame or resentment. The overwhelming mercy of God calls for a "living sacrifice" response. I can't demand that Meeka deny herself for my benefit any more than she can demand that of me. Instead, we trust that each other is giving and sacrificing in response to God's call within the other. The apostle Paul makes this vividly clear with his doxology in Romans 11:33 and Romans 12:1,

> MANY CHRISTIANS HAVE TURNED THE FAMILY, SOMETHING BEAUTIFUL, INTO AN IDOL. MY LOVE FOR MY WIFE AND MY CHILDREN IS NOT ENOUGH. IT WILL FADE AND LEAVE ME AND THE ONES I LOVE IN THE MIDST OF DESTRUCTION. —CS

Oh, the depth of the riches of the wisdom and knowledge of God!

How unsearchable his judgments,
and his paths beyond tracing out!
"Who has known the mind of the Lord?
Or who has ever been his counselor?"
"Who has ever given to God,
that God should repay him?"
For from him and through him and to him are all things.
To him be the glory forever! Amen.

Therefore, I urge you, brothers, in view of God's mercy, to
offer your bodies as living sacrifices, holy and pleasing to God.

The subtle difference between living your life before
God instead of for your husband, wife, or your
ideal family makes the deepest and most significant
difference in a marriage. When one spouse makes
sacrifices in the place of God, the stage is set for
gnawing discontentment. A tidal wave of rage fueled by
frustration and ambivalence will surely surface. I have
spent time with numerous couples that placed their
dreams of having a Christian home and well-adjusted
children above God. When we worship what's moral
and acceptable, even religious, our hearts are blinded
until loneliness and emptiness of our ideals begin to

haunt us. If you doubt what I am saying, open your Bible to the Old Testament prophets. Our biggest problem is rarely atheism. Our hearts are splintered a million different times. We worship the good things, which in turn destroys our homes. The whole reality turns shameful and deadly. People end up hating themselves and each other.

Getting into the idolatrous heart, the Old Testament prophet asks the poignant question: *"To whom do you compare me or count me equal?"*

He goes onto describe the futility of idolatry:

IT SADDENS ME THAT THE DI-VORCE RATE WITHIN THE CHURCH IS SO HIGH. HOWEVER, BILL-BOARDS ANNOUNCING THE NEXT SERMON SERIES AS "FIVE STEPS TO A HAPPY MARRIAGE" ALWAYS DISTURB ME. WHILE I DON'T THINK A HAPPY MARRIAGE OR PLEASING YOUR SPOUSE IS WRONG, IT IS INCOMPLETE AS AN END. MOTIVE MUST ALSO COME INTO QUESTION. OUR EFFORTS TO GIVE MUST ALWAYS BE FOR GOD'S PLEASURE AND PURPOSE.

"Some pour out gold from their bags and weigh out silver on the scales; they hire a goldsmith to make it into a god, And they bow down and worship it. They lift it to their shoulders and carry it; they set it up in its place, and there it stands.

From that spot it cannot move."[3]

By comparison, a "living sacrifice" that responds to God's mercy and calling works into everyday life, making a strong foundation for the years to come. The sort of self-denial of which we speak is possible only through Jesus Christ. For this to happen, each person must continually present their life to God for God's purposes. Cheryl and Gregg had an unspoken agreement to make each other's dreams the thing they lived for. That was their purpose. The wrappings had Jesus' stamps and slogans all over it, but the inside was hollering for happiness and the good life.

The pattern of this world is self-preservation and gratification. This same pattern is often played out within so-called "Christian" homes, wherein the family and happiness become the more acceptable gods

IF YOU THINK YOU ARE A GREAT CATCH FOR SOMEONE, ASK GOD TO BREAK YOU AND WHO YOU ARE IN THE DEPTHS OF YOUR SELFISHNESS. HE WILL ... AND THEN YOU WILL BE A GREAT CATCH. —LS

of choice. Somehow the family has been elevated as the fourth member of the Trinity! This corrupt pattern is firmly planted in this world; it doesn't encourage vulnerability or trust. People who are stuck in this rut are living for fleeting satisfaction; they are trying to stuff the malcontent rising up in their hearts. It doesn't encourage hope in God, but rage against any obstacle or digression. The number one commitment, then, is self-preservation instead of self-denial. We begin this journey with indifference toward God chilling our heart.

Long before we are despairing of our version of the American Dream, we have worshiped God from a safe distance. The frugal worship and miserly offering we have given to God will surely manifest itself in our marriage. The opposite of this sort of malnourished faith is an extravagant life of love, sacrifice, joy, and purpose. An extravagant love, though, isn't possible for a person sinking in insecurity or vanity.

Even more than a wife, Meeka spoke like a true disciple of Jesus Christ. Disciples live in situations causing them to respond to God surprisingly honest: "I don't know if I can trust you! I don't have any other hope!" True worship brings us to the rim of annihilation. Paul's doxology in Romans underscores our absolute dependency upon God, who, in turn, is absolutely self-sufficient. Our stingy lives and stingy love reveal selfish and insecure hearts, grabbing for life like it was up to us. Paul makes it abundantly clear that the only being in the entire universe that is self-sufficient is God. All else is contingent. There isn't a marriage, a happy home, talented children, or a spouse who can compare to God. Our marriage, home, and children, in fact, are more evidence of God's merciful presence in our lives instead of trophies of our well-behaved life. We are called to abandon these small visions of marriage in light of God's grand vision for a God-signifying marriage and relationship. For people who see you and your marriage, it should be like looking through a stained glass that is flooded with the sunlight.

Real Difference

As we become centered on God in our marriages, our eyes are open wide to the way we are to give our hearts sacrificially and joyfully. We are no longer trying to please a spouse or get something from them, but living with eternal purpose. We either live in full view of God's mercy, or we don't really live. And this is the place upon which a husband and wife's marriage must begin: self-denial and living sacrifice. I wanted to take Cheryl and Gregg back to a childlike faith in God. I wanted them to go back to that altar upon which they had promised

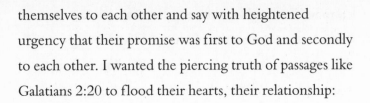
themselves to each other and say with heightened urgency that their promise was first to God and secondly to each other. I wanted the piercing truth of passages like Galatians 2:20 to flood their hearts, their relationship:

> *I have been crucified with Christ ... The life I live in the body, I live by faith in the Son of God.* [4]

The romantic love a man and woman feel for each other isn't a strong enough foundation to live a life of sacrifice. Life will begin to feel like a steep and dangerous mountainside. Your spouse will let you down; their selfish and petty heart will be easily seen. Shame and insecurity will rock the foundation of your commitment. There is only One who deserves your whole life. There is only One who will guide you through those painful places. With the life God hands back to us in Jesus (the life of faith we live), we are then free to pledge to live with another.

Trying times in a marriage measure the authenticity of a couple's ideas and images about marriage. Each time a couple approaches me about counseling before marriage, I can't help but wonder what images and ideas they are bringing to our discussion. What assumptions are just behind their spoken words? In this chapter, we have gotten to the root of one of the most subtle, seemingly natural, albeit self-centered, images: My self-denial is primarily in response to the love I feel for my future spouse. When this goes unchallenged, self-denial turns into rage, hatred, frustration, and resentment. The romantic feelings and the people we love are too fleeting and flawed to make as the object of our life. In the following chapters, we describe marriage as a hopeful challenge to the cynicism of our day. It is a light shining in the darkness. It is light coming from God.

Off the Mountain

Those rocky years in the Mile High city for Meeka and I came to a close with the birth of our first child, Reece. There is not doubt in either one of us that God was preparing us for the renovation and expansion to welcome our first child into our life. Further, there were difficult years ahead of me as a pastor that would necessitate a strong marriage. The destructive and subtle patterns that had matured in the first three years of our marriage had to be faced honestly. I was enrolled in graduate school, and Meeka was working full time.

As Reece's arrival pressed in and as I finished up my studies, Meeka was struggling to trust my lead. She wanted to raise the children she gave birth to, not raise her husband as though he were a child. One of the greatest gifts Meeka gave to me then and continues to give to me in our relationship is her expectation of me as a husband and father. Her decision to trust is a powerful force for good in my life.

To be sure, I have struggled with her lofty expectations, feeling like I couldn't live up to them. I hear a calling within the expectation to be the man God (not Meeka) created me to be. That day on the mountain and the days that followed in those two years, the way I saw the sacrifice act of my love for Meeka fundamentally changed. My life as a husband, and eventually father, was a living sacrifice to God.

DISCUSSION QUESTIONS:

1. What areas of your life are filled with shame and self-contempt? How does vanity rear its ugly head in your relationships? Discuss these questions with your partner.

2. Do you see the differences and the similarities between shame and vanity? Do you understand how they erode a healthy marriage?

3. What parts or images from the story of our hike linger with you? Discuss the need for courage, trust, tenacity, and self-denial in your life and marriage.

4. Give time and space to read Romans 11:33-12:2. A "living sacrifice" in marriage is possible insofar as we see that God's mercy is active throughout our lives. The self-denial is far different from self-hatred or self-absorption. Imagine Paul's doxology in chapter 11 being the lens through which you view everything in your marriage.

5. Consider the following statement from the chapter: "The frugal worship and miserly offering we have given to God will surely manifest itself in our marriage." Note the correlation between worship of God and love of spouse. If we don't love God well, we can't love our spouse well.

6. Read Isaiah 46:6-7. Discuss with your partner ways in which family and marriage can become an idol in your life.

7. Make a list of the very real differences you believe that living unto God in your marriage will make in your life together.

8. The problem isn't that the expectations are too high in relationships, but that expectations are lowered so as to manage desire and to avoid disappointment. Talk a lot about your expectations—the good ones and the ones that aren't so good—with your partner. Many fights are fought over the expectations that need to be spoken and put forth. When you are arguing or you feel disappointed, try to put words to the expectation that was not met.

1. Al Pacino as the Devil in *The Devil's Advocate*

2. Ibid.

3. Isaiah 46:6-7

4. Galatians 2:19-20

"You're here to be light, bringing out the God-colors in the world."

—Matthew 5:14, The Message

5. A SUBTLE REBELLION

The Saturday following September 11, 2001, I (Chad) performed a wedding. People were still talking about the tragedy that punctured America's sense of security. The tragedy was tucked beneath our eyes, behind all of our conversations. But on this sunny Saturday morning, people stopped talking and thinking about the tragedy as they entered the church. As I joined them in the celebration, it seemed to take on the form of a revolt. The conventional imagery and traditional setting was home to a tenacious hope we all carried in our hearts. Evil would not prevail. We would still believe in love and ultimately, God's design for creation.

"Affliction is able to drown out every earthly voice," I began the service, "but the voice of God within a man it cannot." Danish philosopher Søren Kierkegaard isn't usually called upon to set the stage for wedding vows. Given the aftermath, though, the father of existentialism captured the essence of wedding vows poignantly. Kierkegaard, in fact, captured the life of faith in a time and place that seems to undermine faith in anything, much less God. The affliction seems to drown out even the most pious of individuals.

Marriage is a strong fortress. Its cornerstone characteristic is its other-centered posture. Healthy marriages bring life and hope into the world, challenging the despair and cynicism of our day. Marriage affirms hope, faith, and love. Thus, we must see marriage as the city on a hill, the light in a dark of which Jesus spoke. If Jesus thusly describes my life as an individual disciple, then my one-flesh life with my wife is no different.

The Day Before

My wedding ceremony occurred less than a day after my grandfather's death. We received a phone call during our rehearsal dinner. Papa was in his final struggle with cancer in his liver and pancreas. He had been diagnosed with the cancer weeks before his death. With the phone call, Meeka and I jumped into the car and raced to the hospital, our hearts torn in half. Our first day as husband and wife would be my grandparents' first day apart.

Our conversation to and from the hospital was of hard questions. How do you celebrate and grieve? Do we go through with our plans? The timing was all wrong, and nothing seemed to be in its proper place. This is precisely the place where love grows despite the struggle. This is the unromantic, but no less intimate terrain we spoke of a couple of chapters ago. It is in this hostile country where love's real strength shines brightest.

We arrived at the hospital too late. He had died by the time we made it into his room. I don't remember the details of what happened after I stepped into that room. I do remember that his lifeless body looked so different so quickly. It was far removed from the grandfather with the huge smile and fun-loving spirit who we all knew. Immediately my uncle turned to me, his eyes flooded with tears and his voice cracked with emotion, assuring me that tragedy could strengthen a marriage instead of tearing it apart. It was his way of encouraging me to go forward with celebration.

I would have loved for Papa to celebrate with Meeka and me. Papa knew how to have great time. His presence infected all of our family gatherings with fun and laughter. While he was absent the following day, my grandmother graciously came. My uncle and aunt sat on either side of her to comfort her. While I'm thankful that we went through with the celebration, I wish that we had acknowledged the loss and remembered Papa in some way. At some level, though, we lacked the resolve, the faith—seen in the Psalms, for instance—to mix our grief and celebration. Psalm 84 is a good example of worship and celebration arising out of disappointment and struggle:

> *My soul years, even faints*
> *For the courts of the Lord;*
> *My heart and my flesh cry out*
> *For the living God.*

As in the case of this psalm, one of the most powerful

weapons one has in the face of difficulty is hope; the honest expression of desire in the face of great disappointment becomes a tenacious refusal to give in to despair. Our wedding plans were carried out because of my family's hope. Even in the wake of Papa's death, we believed that the "one flesh" being born that day was reason to celebrate.

My one regret is that we would have strived to put words to our loss as we celebrated the expansion of our family. I'm not even sure how we could have done such a thing. Having people remember out loud the legacy Papa had left would have been powerful. The key in that situation would have been to remember. Throughout the Old Testament, the ancient Hebrews would, in the face of trying times, remember the blessings of God in their midst. Though situations threatened to silence their communal voice, they spoke of God's gracious and powerful presence in their midst.

A Song in Babylon

The fact that this understanding is missing in most wedding celebrations is a reflection on the state of communal worship in Church as a whole. The collection of prayers and songs in the book of Psalms belies our shallow worship. There are numerous Psalms of disorientation preceding celebrations of God's order. "It is no wonder that the church has intuitively avoided these psalms. They lead us into dangerous acknowledgement of how life really is. They lead us into the presence of God where everything is not polite and civil."[1] The Psalms are a living, faith-filled response. This collection of ancient prayers and petitions, of worship and liturgy captures the tension I have felt at every wedding I've ever attended but that is talked about so little.

Take Psalm 137, a song composed while the people are in exile.

> *By the rivers of Babylon we sat and wept*
> *when we remembered Zion.*
> *There on the poplars*
> *we hung our harps ...*
> *How can we sing the songs of the Lord*
> *while in a foreign land?*

How do we sing in the face of a reality that mocks our

celebration? There isn't a ceremonial plan to be strictly followed or seven steps. That's not what the Psalms reveal. How we sing the songs in the face of chaos may look differently in different places and in different times. I'm not sure what a hope-filled, living response always looks like. I just know that it must happen.

While the September 11th circumstances were as unique as they were colossal, I don't normally think of weddings all that differently. Weddings go off every day surrounded by divorce, death, angry family members, and other less than ideal settings. Pretending otherwise or pandering to the chaos is unacceptable. The former persists in naïveté, choosing to sing sweeter songs instead. It lacks substance and real faith. The latter lacks faith too, ruled by despair and cynicism.

Since I was very young and understood the fact that people divorce and die unexpectedly, weddings always struck me as either terribly naïve or a waste. My thinking has evolved; wedding days are occasions for a hopeful response to the cynical tides carrying people into lives of despairing loneliness and fleeting gratification. Our persistent belief and extraordinary effort spent on symbols and celebration for wedding vows, properly understood, is an extravagant celebration of what God intended for man and woman. Having stripped much of our weekly worship services of symbols and the sacred space that our faith fathers and mothers seemed to protect, we have, according to Stanley Hauerwas, "given atheists less and less to disbelieve."[2]

As a pastor, I take my role of speaking into the community of faith very seriously. At a very basic level, I am called to describe and call out God's mysterious ways among us. (We'll talk more about this in another chapter.) My role as pastor, though, also brings me to the forefront of heartache and tragedy. "The good therapist fights darkness and seeks illumination, while romantic love is sustained by mystery and crumbles upon inspection. I hate to be love's executioner."[3] I take up arms where promise and hope collide head-on with reality and mockery. As we will see later, the pastor's words matter for this very important illumination.

Despite the darkness I have witnessed in my short life, I still believe that people can promise a life to each other and fulfill that promise. But this hope, to be sure, has been severely tested. Several years back, it was like we took a front seat to what felt like an epidemic of infidelity. Meeka and I heard painful stories from people we loved and cared for who were either going through or had been through marital infidelity. We wondered if any commitment was immune from this crushing blow.

The evidence spoke a loud and clear, "No." Any marriage is susceptible to betrayal. No one has the luxury of lulling themselves into believing that they have somehow moved past that possibility. Meeka and I found ourselves talking and struggling with this harsh reality. This environment wasn't friendly to the vows we had spoken, "till death do us part." While there were no foolproof safeguards, we arrived at hope.

"Is it naïve for me to think that we could possibly live fifty years together and not have to live through this heartache?" Meeka wondered aloud.

"No," I replied. "That is called hope." Our hope rests in the truth that God will finish what He started in our hearts. Left to our own self-discipline, our odds for decades of trust and fidelity diminish greatly.

Instead of reclining in the seat of mockers on wedding days and taking bets on when the vows will crumble, I stand with couples or join them in the congregation, believing that the marriage will confront the prevailing winds in our culture. I believe, despite evidence to the contrary, a couple can fulfill their vows by hoping in God.

Can you imagine?

While Meeka and I were living through this heartache, God was fashioning a renewed vision of marriage. As we laid out in chapter one, marriage is depicted in Genesis and substantiated in the teachings of Jesus. "We need to ask not whether it is realistic or practical or viable but whether it is imaginable," Walter Brueggemann said.[4] Scripture invites us to imagine a life centered in God. Meeka's question got to the heart of the issue:

I WAS TERRIBLY SADDENED BY THE RELATIONAL LANDSCAPE IN WHICH WE WERE LIVING. PEOPLE I LOVED AND TRUSTED, PEOPLE I LOOKED TO AND HOPED WITH WERE IN DESPERATE PLACES; THEY SEEMED HOPELESS. I COULDN'T HELP BUT WONDER IF THERE WERE ANY WARNING SIGNS WE WERE MISSING. YET, I FELT CLOSER AND MORE INTIMATE TO HIM. WE WERE STRENGTHENED DURING THE DIFFICULT PERIOD. —MK

whether or not we should lower our expectations from

the vows we had made. The images in the Bible hold the bar in place. Scripture paints a vivid picture of lifelong promise and trust. This sacred text is God's primary instrument through which our imaginations are fueled to re-imagine life, relationships, and the world in which we live.

Who has time to imagine? We don't read and meditate on Scripture. It's got to make sense, and it's got to work like some kind of new drug. Well meaning Christians have been co-opted by a voracious demand that things make sense ... now. "Our culture is competent to implement almost anything," continues Brueggemann, "and to imagine almost nothing." Without a compelling vision there is little hope for survival. Vision fuels hope.

The images of matrimony many well-meaning newlywed couples begin with are small, hopeless, or lack substance; they are more deeply rooted in personal history and earthly treasures than faith. A biblical portrait is lavish. According to Scripture, a couple lives without shame, vulnerable, and in the full view of God's pleasure. This image has been overwhelmed by images of fiscal responsibility, growing 2.5 kids, and saving for

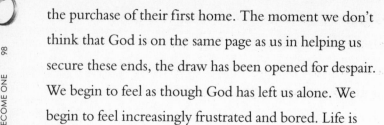

the purchase of their first home. The moment we don't think that God is on the same page as us in helping us secure these ends, the draw has been opened for despair. We begin to feel as though God has left us alone. We begin to feel increasingly frustrated and bored. Life is lackluster.

It's little wonder that we are unable to implement a worshipful, God-honoring relationship—we haven't really imagined it to be so. A couple who bucks the status quo and chooses, instead, of thinking of their marriage biblically, begins to awaken to "learn the unforced rhythms of grace" (Matthew 11).

God created us so that if we place our minds on something over a long period of time, we begin to live out the mental picture. Professor Dallas Willard makes this point clear:

"Our thoughts are one of the most basic sources of our life. They determine the orientation of everything we do and evoke the feelings that frame our world and motivate our actions. Interestingly, you can't evoke thoughts by feeling a certain way, but you can evoke and to some degree control feelings by directing your thoughts. Our power over our thoughts is of great and indispensable assistance in directing and controlling our feelings ... We cannot just choose our feelings."[5]

Willard's teaching points the way for an engaged or newlywed couple. Before you are fighting over how you feel, a couple should be very open and honest about what ideas and thoughts are acting as the "source" material for their relationship. Individually, a husband and wife must continue in the redemption of their thoughts (the ideas and images governing their lives) until their minds are patterned after a consuming passion for God's glory. With thoughts being continually fed by the images in Scripture of God's magnificent power, transcendence, and immanence, the arguments, the irritations, the children, the money, the new home, and all the other

TAKE SPECIFIC TIME TO IMAGINE YOUR LIFE TOGETHER. DON'T JUST FOCUS ON WHAT YOU *DON'T* WANT TO BECOME; LOOK BEYOND THE NEGATIVE AND SEE SOMETHING LIFE-GIVING; IMAGINE WHAT YOU *WILL* BECOME. SHARE THE SECRET DESIRES OF YOUR HEART WITH EACH OTHER EARLY ON AND KNOW THAT THOSE BECOME STRONGHOLDS FOR GOOD IN YOUR MARRIAGE DOWN THE ROAD. —CK

nitty-gritty details of a couple's life is impacted. Flowing from this rich imagination is God-centered living.

Seeing your spouse as an ally and your marriage as a stronghold for God's purpose places your relationship face-to-face with prevailing cynicism and the eternal hope you will need. "God's intention is for our spouses to be our allies—intimate friends, lovers, warriors ... We are to draw strength, nourishment, and courage to fight well from that one person who most deeply supports and joins us in the wars—our soul mate for life."[6]

Moreover, that image of life on earth, marriage, is deeply rooted in our ancestry. Of our father of faith, Abraham, Paul wrote, "Against all hope, Abraham in hope believed and so became the father of many nations, just as it had been said to him ... he did not waver through unbelief regarding the promise of God, but was strengthened in his faith and gave glory to God, being fully persuaded that God had power to do what he had promised" (Romans 4:18, 20-21).

Abraham, though his life was filled with struggles— some he handled well and some he botched—was illumined by a vision of God's promise of a son and of a country. Similarly, a newly married couple must seek the same illumined vision of their life. For images of such a life, see Hebrews 11. Spend time reading this chapter together as a couple. Spend time alone, away from each other, reading through this chapter. Ask the Spirit to open your eyes to its "foolishness," and so seek to live a similar life as husband and wife.

New Vision—New Life

Swirling around in any argument between a husband and wife are powerful images and emotions that are fueled by past experiences and relationship. Parenting, moreover, is similarly connected to images we carry around in our subconscious for years. Our experiences down through the years can have a profound impact on the here and now. If we are not watchful, false images and volatile emotions can bring about severe damage to a relationships.

As people saved by grace through faith in Jesus Christ, our minds have the power to take captive thoughts and feelings that are misguided and rooted in definitive moments from our past. This will not happen automatically, though; we must be actively involved in this process.

We're not mere victims of a liberal, anti-family, amoral agenda. Marriage and life are like battles; they are battles for our spirits and minds. The apostle Paul knew this and pleaded with the Romans to see themselves as more than conquerors.

No, in all of these things we are more than conquerors through him who loved us. For I am convinced that [nothing] will be able to separate us from the love of God that is in Christ Jesus our Lord.[7]

Scripture calls us outward, not inward. An authentic love relationship bears witness to God's intentions and design for marriage. Today's environment is at the least indifferent toward love and at worst mocking. It would be dangerously naïve for two people to vow their lives to each other in a romantic ceremony and live unaware of their harsh surroundings. Their destruction would be only a matter of time.

While Scripture teaches us that marriage will fade into

non-existence in the afterlife, for now it is a powerful affront in a world of disbelief and skepticism. The disbelief is first and foremost a disbelief in God. But every couple is susceptible to a loss of vision and belief in what God has ordained. No one is immune from being negatively impacted by the surroundings.

In the chapter that follows, we will explore a very practical and subversive step for a young marriage. We'll uncover the rich history of a "sacred first year." During that the first year of marriage, a couple can establish the image and patterns that will be powerful influences for years to come.

DISCUSSION QUESTIONS:

1. What's the scene going to be like on your wedding? What tragedy or hopelessness will be mixed in with the celebration? Are there failed marriages in the crowd?

2. How does your trust relationship challenge cynicism of our day?

3. While surely your marriage will be a source of deep

satisfaction, what do you think of your marriage being more than just self-satisfying? What sort of vision of marriage is this chapter depicting? God introduces pleasure and satisfaction with Eve.

4. Look back at Dallas Willard's paragraph about the importance of choosing our thoughts that impact our feelings. Pay special attention to the following sentence from that quote: "Interestingly, you can't evoke thoughts by feeling a certain way, but you can evoke and to some degree control feelings by directing your thoughts." Why is this such an important truth in marriage?

5. What images of marriage haunt you? What mental images fuel fear and undermine the hope needed for trust and fidelity? Where are these images rooted?

6. There is no immunity, only hope. What is the difference between being immune to betrayal and hope in the face of struggles? Our hope is the persistent and redemptive love of God. See Romans 8:37-39.

7. Read Psalm 84. Note the voice of hope and tenacious refusal to give into despair.

1. Walter Brueggemann, *The Message of the Psalms: A Theological Commentary*, (Augsburg: Minneapolis, 1984), 53.

2. Hauerwas, Stanley and Willimon, H. William, *Resident Aliens: Life in the Christian Colony*, (Abingdon: Nashville, 1989), 50.

3. Yalom, Iriving, *Love's Executioner*, (HarperCollins: New York, 1989), 15.

4. Brueggemann, Walter, *The Prophetic Imagination*, (Fortress Press, 1978), 45.

5. Dallas Willard, *Renovation of the Heart: Putting on the Character of Christ*, (Colorado Springs: NavPress, 2002), 96.

6. Allender, Dan and Longman, Tremper, *Intimate Allies*, (Tyndale: Wheaton, 1995) xvi.

7. Romans 8:37-39

"Therefore I am now going to allure her. I will lead her into the desert and speak tenderly to her. There I will give her back her vineyards."

—Hosea 1:14-15, NIV

6. A SACRED YEAR

Psychology is an inexact science. It is impossible to predict human behavior. There is not a pre-marital test, psychologist, pastor, or counselor that can predict how either you or your spouse will respond to one another in years to come. I (Chris) stood on stage as the best man in the wedding of a dear friend almost a decade ago. This wedding was near perfect, if there is such a thing; the flower bill alone was likely equal to my student loans. His bride possessed a rare and breathtaking beauty, and I had never seen her look better. The reception was a celebration of what God had done in bringing them together. I was intoxicated by the emotion that surrounded the two of them. As I write this, they have a divorce in progress. Weeks before the birth of their second child, my friend disappeared—missing his own daughter's birth. He was apparently riding motorcycles with a new girlfriend as his baby girl entered the world with an absent father. In a million years, I would have never guessed he was capable of ignoring his vows and shunning his own children.

It is all too common. One of my childhood-friends-turned-country-music-star was getting so consumed with his blossoming career he began to pay no attention to his wife/childhood sweetheart. Though we were good friends, he stopped returning my calls. As I boarded a plane in the Phoenix airport, I was astounded to see his wife on my plane. When I asked her where she was going, the tears began to pour. She was on her way home to sign their divorce papers. The same man who proclaimed his eternal love to her in song on their wedding day was in the shower with another woman when she came home early from work a few months earlier. There was no repentance nor apologies, only resignation to his selfish path.

How did these kind, loving, and seemingly devoted
husbands get from Point A to Point B? I don't know.
And truth be told, I am filled with anger at both of
them. If they had just been honest, asked for help, and
pushed through the hard times, they could have avoided
this heartbreak. I do not know how they got there,
but I know how they could have avoided it. We can't
predict our future, but we are creatures of habit. Our
rituals become powerful predictors of what is to come.
My challenge to you is to create some rituals that don't
invite this kind of devastation. Build walls of protection
around your union by making intimacy a natural part of
each day.

Nothing Good is Easy

Marriage, my friends, is hard work. The simple truth
is that if you do not devote yourself completely to it,
you will fail. You don't believe me? Do you think your
relationship can weather the storms that come with
divided loyalties? Some may stay together, but they settle
for a cheap substitute. Real biblical marriage is where
two become one. No divisions. No secrets. No excuses.
Just complete and total oneness.

God knew that this kind of oneness would not happen automatically, so in His supreme wisdom, He ordered that all newlyweds should set aside their first year of marriage as an extended honeymoon, a relational boot camp, and a time of consecration to God and one another. We are creatures of habit, and the patterns you set in dating and in your early years of marriage will either be a blessing or a curse. You may take a moment every night before you fade off to sleep to look one another in the eyes, and from your honeymoon to your fiftieth anniversary, it will become a natural part of your day. Or you may begin to belittle you spouse for little things that annoy you (their reckless driving, snoring, or naiveté), and every day the chasm between the two of you will grow wider. As Peter Cetera (of the '80s ballad band Chicago) once sang, *habits are hard to break*, so start some good ones.

God's law still applies to us today. Its principles remain true. In Deuteronomy, God's law says, "When a man takes a new wife, he is not to go out with the army or be given any business or work duties. He gets one year off simply to be at home making his wife happy."[1] Imagine that—a yearlong honeymoon! No work, social obligations, or responsibilities. Just an entire year for food, wine, laughter, and lots of sex. No couple in their right mind would pass that up—all of a sudden the Old Testament law sounds great. (So you have to sacrifice animals every now and then. But, you get a year off to eat great food and develop your bedroom skills.) A fifty-two week vacation is usually impossible for newlyweds in our culture, but the importance of the sacred year is not diminished.

This book is about how you can create an environment for your marriage to thrive. It is a guidebook for your sacred year. Your first year of marriage may be like paradise, or, like mine, it may be very hard. Either way, you can set a foundation that will make your marriage strong if you commit together to settle for nothing less than biblical oneness. You must figure out how to contextualize the truth of this historic command to your own circumstances. So let's examine the environment for your sacred year.

QUALITY OR QUANTITY TIME?

There is no substitute for time together. There are

many forces in your lives that will seek to separate the two of you—work, travel schedules, old friends, family, school, laziness, or even church activities. In my first year of marriage, it was the numerous invitations for me to travel to speak at conferences and conventions. The income that these trips provided would be very helpful for our young family, but the time we would spend apart could prove to be more costly. As Lisa and I considered what we could do to create a sacred year, we decided that we would not spend a night separated during our first year. If someone wanted me to speak at an event, they would also have to pay for my wife to come as well. If I did not speak anywhere that year, then we would find a way to make ends meet. To my surprise, nearly everyone was happy to invest in my marriage. Lisa and I traveled to San Diego, San Francisco, Washington D.C., Philadelphia, Chicago, and many other cities that year, usually adding extra days to see the sites or relax by a hotel pool. Little did we know that this would be the saving grace of our marriage during this fragile time.

ENEMIES OF ONENESS

There are infinite sources for problems in marriage.

For Lisa and I, it was our strong wills and independent spirits that made marriage so hard in the beginning. There were no simple solutions for the constant tension we muddled through that first year. It could have vanished if I had a humbler spirit that rushed headlong into confession and repentance instead of clinging to justification. The fact that we walked through these issues together made us stronger and led us to trust instead of isolation.

It is important that you identify the forces that seek to separate you and find some ways to be intentional about spending time together. These questions are intended to help you on that path:

Are both of you employed? Is travel involved, or are long hours expected? Can one of you take a leave of absence or choose not to work? How can you set your schedule to maximize your time together?

Beware of old friends or family that undermine your relationship. If your job is demanding or other factors have the ability to drive a wedge between you, what routines can you establish in the first year to make one another a priority?

Can you do one or more of the following: Spend every night together, share a meal once a day, plan romantic dates for twice a week, schedule weekly lunch-hour picnics, establish a bedtime routine of interaction, spend every Saturday together, or choose to read the same books and discuss them daily?

It begins with time spent together, but it doesn't end there.

Conflict

Conflict is inevitable. When I'm walking through pre-marital counseling with a couple, I want to know how they fight. If you haven't had a good fight, then go have one, because I won't marry you until you do. The way you deal with conflict resolution can be either a saving grace or a fatal flaw to marriage. I had a lot to learn.

I had a mistress during my first year of marriage: Her name was pride, and I became unwilling to sacrifice for my bride. My long-term affair could have become like a cancer destroying the soul of my emerging family. I loved "being right," and I loved her much more than my wife. I am not always right—but I want to be. I thought good husbands were right, so I fought for my point of view and lobbied for my position. All the while my bride was dying inside. Eventually my wife was battered by my fight club mentality (debating driving directions, blaming, and looking for victory). She couldn't withstand the blows, and I finally learned I was losing by winning. Here are some important issues to consider:

Do you deal with conflict well? Do you deal with conflict at all? Have either of you ever been involved in an abusive relationship of any kind? What tendencies do you bring to the relationship that makes conflict difficult? Do you keep your composure and manage your temper but plan to go ten rounds?

Are you willing to break the tension to pray, hug, and cool off? Will both of you lay down your pride to make real peace? Can you admit it is possible that you are in the wrong?

Do you suppress your anger or avoid conflict? Do you give off signals that you are upset but not verbally communicate your feelings?

Make a plan for how you will deal with conflict. Set some rules and a parachute clause. If you cannot find resolution, choose someone whom you will call for prayer and counsel (i.e., a pastor or mentoring couple).

Money and Sex

Sex and money are known as the two most divisive issues in marriage. But in reality, they are only indicators of problems that already exist. If you are struggling in either of these areas, it reveals that some priorities are out of whack. If you are accumulating debt, it reveals problems of selfishness, impatience, or a lust for immediate gratification. Talk about your finances and sex life with complete honesty and candor on a regular basis. What patterns can you create in these areas that help you set patterns that are healthy?

Do you tithe? Do you give to others generously? Do you accumulate debt by spending beyond your income? Do you save?

Discuss your previous financial mistakes and ways you can help one another. What financial goals can you set for your family? Can you buy a house and avoid the financial pitfall of renting?

Are you in relationship with other couples that offer you wisdom and insight? Is there anyone you submit to?

God has made us to be creatures of habit. We thrive on rhythms that guide us through the chaos that hovers over us all. So, the Creator has mandated times of focus for mankind. Taking a Sabbath day each week is a part of that rhythm. Push yourselves into the patterns that will help you flourish. A friend has developed a ritual he enjoys every night with his wife (except occasions they might be traveling). As they prepare for bed, he draws a bath for his wife, and then he sits on the toilet engaging a lengthy conversation as she bathes. While she dries off, he takes a short bath. They crawl into bed and make love before they fall asleep. It has become the most important, relaxing, and restful part of their day. For more than forty years, they have held to this simple schedule and left very little opportunity for the two of them to grow apart. Oneness won't happen by accident. Your union must be planted in soil that will protect it, nourish it, and strengthen it for the storms that are always around the corner.

It is difficult to let anger and resentment fester while you share, laugh, and bathe with your spouse. Pour all you have in to this union and enjoy the fruits of your love for an entire lifetime.

DISCUSSION QUESTIONS:

1. Before you consider how to balance life's demands and your new or potential marriage, what balance can you find in your personal life? What things need to be included or excluded?

2. What routines can be established in the first year to make one another a priority? What routines need to be interrupted?

3. If both you and your spouse will be working, how will your workload impact your marriage? Is there any adjustments in employment and/or work patterns that need to be made?

4. What is my pattern of behavior in conflict? Am I annoyed or really disappointed and afraid? What is the source of my disappointment or fear? Was there honest and honoring conversation?

5. Discuss your previous financial mistakes and strategic ways you can help one another. Do you accumulate debt by spending beyond your income? Do you give to others generously? Do you save?

1. Deuteronomy 24:5 (MES)

"At its roots, the hunger for food is the hunger for survival. At its roots, the hunger to know a person sexually is the hunger to know and be known by that person humanly. Food without nourishment doesn't fill the bill for long, and neither does sex without humanness."

—Frederick Buechner, *Wishful Thinking*

7. A SACRED SPACE

Meeka and I took things very slow at the outset of our relationship. And while we had waited some time before our first kiss, once we were engaged, the God-given desire to take the next step in intimacy flourished with full force. The closer our wedding day drew near, the harder we had to work at not climbing into bed together. We took great care to avoid situations that would lead us to the bedroom. Wedding plans, family, and future unknowns were compelling reasons to save our sexual union until after the vows were spoken. We wanted to start in the right place, heading in the right direction. More than simply wanting to be good, though, we started slow because of past mistakes. It was obvious that something very special had begun in our relationship, and we didn't want to sabotage it with our lack of self-restraint. We talked a lot during this time. We talked with each other about past sins and sorted through the residue of pain, guilt, and shame. In an effort to start afresh, we skied together, took walks, spent time with friends, and got to know one another over long conversations.

We were forging a very strong emotional connection. Too often mistakes are made, both in and out of marriage, because physical intimacy becomes an end in and of itself. It is the scratch that satisfies an itch. Understood properly, the sexual union a couple enjoys is an expression of the bond they share. So much of my own failures in the area of sexuality had to do with misunderstanding this principle. I had belittled the gift God had given to me in the area of my sexual desire. I had squandered the desire like an ignorant child.

Mystery, Beauty

On their album *Slow Dark Train*, Bill Mallonee and the Vigilantes of Love (VOL) included a track that eventually led to the loss of a record deal. The album, along with the track in question, was eventually issued on Capricorn Records. The following is from the song "Love Cocoon":

Honey, I wanna attack your flesh, with glad abandon
I wanna look for your fruits, I wanna put my hands on 'em
I wanna pump your thermostat, beneath your skin
I wanna uncover your swimming hole and dive right in

I'm a moth when I fly, when I fly to the light of my doom
You wrap me up in your
love, love cocoon

THIS IS SO SACRED IN OUR RELATIONSHIP, SUCH PRIVATE AND INTIMATE SPACE. THIS AREA OF OUR RELATIONSHIP IS THE ONE AREA THAT NEITHER OF US SHARES WITH ANY OTHER PERSON. IT IS A WONDERFUL GIFT FROM GOD THAT DESERVES A YOUNG COUPLE'S FULL ATTENTION. IT MUST BE CARED FOR AND CULTIVATED. IT DOESN'T HAPPEN AUTOMATICALLY. —MK

I highly recommend you get a copy of this VOL album. I think it portrays the Christian culture's awkward dance with one of God's most unblushingly beautiful and pleasurable creations. Local churches and communities are full of married couples experiencing struggles—not the least of which is occurring in the bedroom—and yet there is virtually nothing all that helpful for these couples.

Mallonee's passion plea in "Love Cocoon" reminds me of a much older and provocative song. The Song of Songs boldly contains Solomon's celebration of God's design between a man and woman. Yet, it is given short and poorly interpreted shrift in most churches.

> *The feelings I get when I see the high mountain ranges*
> *—stirrings of desire, longings for the heights—*
> *Remind me of you,*
> *And I'm spoiled for anyone else!*
> *Your beauty within and without, is absolute,*
> *Dear lover, close companion.*
> *You are tall and supple, like the palm tree,*
> *And your full breasts are like sweet clusters of dates.*
> *I say, "I'm going to climb that palm!*
> *I'm going to caress its fruit!"*
> *Oh yes! Your breasts*
> *Will be clusters of sweet fruit to me.*[1]

As a pastor, I consider the crux of my job resting not so much in telling people what to avoid, but in painting vivid pictures of living for God's glory, in God's design.

It has more to do with cultivating vision in people, with regard to, say, their sexuality, and less about keeping them from doing the wrong thing. Recall the haunting words we mentioned earlier of C.S. Lewis, which are as unusual as they are refreshing in Christendom: "It would seem that our Lord finds our desires not too strong, but too weak. We are half-hearted creatures ..."[2]

Couples in their middle years, who are still trying to fight the boredom and fleeting fantasies of another's bedroom, heard very little about the truth in sexual union when they began, which points to the Church's

IF TRUE LOVE DOESN'T WAIT, TRUE LOVE FORGIVES! —LS

impoverished imagination and understanding concerning God's design and intention.

If you didn't know any better, you would think that sexual intimacy is an evil concoction that had to be secretly enjoyed by God-fearing Christians. Efforts like True Love Waits and much of the talk about sexual purity pave the way for pharisaical righteousness—and if not self-righteousness, then people who fail to live up to the credos are imprisoned in guilt, worried if they will ever enjoy beautiful sex with a future spouse.

All but ignored, Solomon's Song would spark a boy or girl's imagination, sure, but it might also begin to reveal the level of maturity and enjoyment that is unsustainable in a relationship outside of a marriage commitment. Don't get me wrong. The commitment in marriage is the place for the gift of sex to be enjoyed. But more often than not, the Christian ghetto campaigns for self-enhancement through sexual abstinence creates a cult of virginity.

THE LEVEL OF SHAMELESS ENJOY-MENT A COUPLE EXPERIENCES IS DIRECTLY PROPORTIONAL TO THE STRENGTH OF THE RELATIONSHIP. —LS

There is a fundamental flaw in such campaigns. As in every area of life, acts of transgression in a person's sexuality always stem from deeper problems than the acts themselves. Sexual intimacy is either another living sacrificial act of worship in God's design, or it is a selfish act of self-serving idolatry. The perversion that may surface in these areas has more to do with the great exchange that Paul describes in Romans 1 than with what we view as the unseemly acts. The real perversion, as is the case with everything that is good and beautiful in the universe, is when we are consuming God's creation for our appetites instead of living for His glory:

"What happened was this: People knew God perfectly well, but when they didn't treat him like God, refusing to worship him, they trivialized themselves into silliness and confusion so that there was neither sense nor direction left in their lives. They pretended to know it all, but were illiterate regarding life. They traded the glory of God who holds the whole world in his hands for cheap figurines you can buy at any roadside stand."[3]

The embarrassment of feeling like you know too little or too much of the shame rooted in past sins will ultimately derail a healthy relationship, especially in the bedroom. Of all the issues a couple faces, those within the bedroom stand to reveal the most about what is essential in a healthy marriage. A deep-seeded trust, matched with a shameless enjoyment of each other, not only make the bedroom the beautiful refuge God intended, but they are essential to a strong relationship. This chapter will attempt to negotiate the glorious and often misunderstood shorelines of one of God's most beautiful creations: sexual intimacy between a man and woman.

By calling upon personal experiences and looking into God's Word, we hope to offer practical, real-life insight.

No matter if you have been single for sometime, decades removed from any such virginity campaigns, or fresh out of high school, it is pivotal to grapple with this issue. Whether you are married or looking forward to marriage, the unblushing pleasure meant for you and your spouse is for God's glory. With that in mind, I think of the astute observation made by characters in Fyodor Dostoevsky's novel *Brothers Karamazov*: "Beauty is not only a terrible thing; it is also a mysterious thing. There God and the Devil strive for mastery, and the battleground is the heart of men."

Every honest couple must face the beauty of their sexuality in all of its terrible mystery. A healthy sexual relationship between a man and woman rests upon the pillars of Jesus' Gospel. Two people must cling to the redemption of Jesus Christ, be committed to extravagantly seeking the other's pleasure, while being free to explore new territory together.

Meeka and I met soon after high school. When I saw her for the first time, her long, curly, blond hair and blue eyes left me reeling. I had a hard time keeping my mind on school; I could barely think of much else beyond when I would see her next. She was beautiful, and I, as Paul so aptly describes, was "burning" with desire.

Fourteen years later, her face and body, along with the beauty stemming from her soul, have aged like a truly fine wine. We sometimes joke about how many times we have had sex and all of the experiences we have had together. We laugh at how innocent and intense our desire was for each other in those early days and how it has matured. Without a doubt, the love making that we enjoy now, nearly thirteen years later, is far better and more satisfying. The trial and errors and the honest feedback have made the journey worthwhile. We are still growing; we still make mistakes, and the fundamental need for redemption, extravagance, and freedom are required.

Redemption

Young or old, no one shows on their wedding day
perfectly clean without blemish. Our courtship included
getting to know each other; we were sharing with each
other the stuff we would rather keep tucked away in the
past. We arrived in each other's presence bandaged and
tattered. We were the victims of other people's sin; we
had also made bad decisions along the way.

In fact, part of my struggle had to do with the selfish
expectations I was imposing upon Meeka. Looking back
on those days, I was an awful human being, spurning
Meeka when she had been completely honest. There
were several occasions in which she would have been
totally justified had she turned away from me and
never looked back. She deserved so much more. The
fact that she didn't is testimony to her beauty and
the grace of God that was flooding into her heart.
Meeka's transformation at that time in her life steadily
dismantled my arrogance. I was totally duplicitous in
my expectations too. Before Meeka entered my life,
I had made my share of mistakes in relationship. An
inadequate understanding of what God had done with
my tattered and torn past showed up in how I treated

Meeka concerning the mistakes she had made and the hurt she had experienced.

I was young and naïve. I had grown up in the Church with right and wrong behavior pounded into my head; however, my understanding of forgiveness and redemption and the hope therein was shallow at best. My ignorance about human sexuality and the renewal that was possible in Christ was hurting Meeka. While we weathered that time together and eventually made vows to each other, it was three years into our marriage before I realized the level of hurt I had inflicted upon her. I finally had perspective that allowed me to see my own arrogant actions; I also saw in a new light the beauty Meeka possessed as a result of God's work in her life. I was more attracted to her at that time than I had been at any other time in our relationship. "One of the most fundamental and important tasks that has been entrusted to marriage is the work of reclaiming the body for the Lord, of making pure and clean and holy again that which had been trampled in the mud of shame."[4]

To be sure, the love we now enjoy, in and out of the bedroom, is a fragrant offering in our home; it is pointing others to God. We live fully aware of God's redemptive work in our life. I have friends who handled their sexuality with more integrity and purity before they married. They look back with their spouses with different feelings and responses, I'm sure. Meeka and I look into that area of our past and see God working in spite of mistakes and selfishness. Like so many of the Psalms, our memories are like songs where our struggle is evident but God's grace is center stage. Our love making is song. And that is the song of songs.

The root in sexual sin and the ensuing shame that fills the soul has little to do with the physical act itself and involves the betrayal of creation. Paul made clear that "men have turned away and worship the creation instead of the creator." We must deal with the situation many of us face during engagement and courtship at a level of idolatry and forgiveness. Jesus warned the Pharisees that cleaning the outside of the cup was useless. Christ must address the seed of corruption.

The act of sexual sin is always rooted in a violent spirit of selfishness. The appetite for sex-on-demand can slowly turn into a consuming addiction. Sexual addiction "is a byproduct of loneliness, pain, the self-centered contempt to be loved and accepted regardless of the consequences, and loss of vital relationship with God."[5] As the years wear on and the wounds fester, it doesn't matter whether the history of the sin manifested in bisexuality, Internet pornography, or multiple partners. The key to redemption is receiving Christ into the area of violence that rejects God's sovereignty.

EXTRAVAGANCE

"Extravagant love is only possible to the degree that I am lost in His lavish love."[6] The author of a poignant article recalls the words of Teresa of Avila and the fountain of love that overflows out of the believing soul: "May I be mad with love for Him, who for love of me became mad." Indeed, the extravagant and thus risky love made and shared in the bedroom must be deeply rooted and hoping in the love of

DON'T TAKE LIFE—OR SEX—TOO SERIOUSLY. LAUGH, LOVE, AND EXPERIMENT WILDLY. YOU HAVE NOTHING TO LOSE. —CS

God as shown in Jesus Christ. While we were infidels, running after other Gods, Christ died for us.

After God dealt graphically and indignantly with Israel's sin, he spoke extravagant love into the unfaithful people through Hosea:

And now, here's what I'm going to do:
I'm going to start all over again.
I'm taking her back out into the wilderness
Where we had our first date, and I'll court her.
I'll give her bouquets of roses.
I'll turn her Heartbreak Valley into Acres of Hope.
She'll respond like she did as a young girl,
Those days when she was fresh out of Egypt.[7]

Having cultivated a redemptive environment, a couple can make extravagant love, sharing freely from the hope they have in God. Expressions of love are shared in the face of possibly being rejected, being found lacking, or looking like a fool. Running that risk is part of being in love; it is what lovers do when they are in love. From the outsider's perspective, love always has a shade of foolishness in its most profound expression. Look at God's love with unfaithful Israel.

In the bedroom, a couple's expression of their love

and selflessness ranges in possibilities. From oral sex to sharing erotic thoughts concerning each other, to massages to different and new techniques, all is part of extravagant lovemaking. All are grounded in an environment that takes the Gospel seriously. Our extravagant worship of God gives way to creative beauty and extravagance in our marriage. Conversely, couples afraid and inhibited in the bedroom have yet to take a big gulp of God's salvation in their sexuality. Salvation sets us free indeed—in every area of life. Shame keeps us locked into a meaningless struggle, starving us from a satisfying life that God has for us.

Shame, on the other hand, is the silent killer smothering initiative and creativity. Unchecked, shame

> THERE ARE CERTAINLY TIMES LEADING UP TO INTERCOURSE THAT AREN'T OVERLY ROMANTIC. THE SEXUAL UNION WE ENJOY, THOUGH, REFLECTS SOMETHING DEEPER THAN THE MOMENT ITSELF. IT REFLECTS THE BOND WE SHARE. AND GIVING EXPRESSION TO THAT BOND DEEPENS OUR INTIMACY. IT HAS TO! —MK

whispers doubts into the ear of a lover, undermining the confidence he or she can stand on in Christ. Like cracks in a falling structure, so these doubts begin to show up in various areas of the relationship. Shame squelches the initiative and creativity that lovemaking requires.

Shame convinces its victim to cover up, to stay within unrealistic boundaries, and to stay away from risking something new. Shame is a prison.

Freedom

Redemption doesn't erase the past. It changes the way we see the past and, thus, how we see the present and future.

Open lines of communication in the bedroom and during the act of making love are powerful weapons that keep things real. Yet talking about each other's dreams, concerns, desires, misgivings, and disappointments can feel terribly awkward. We have been conditioned by a relentless and subtle bombardment upon our minds. We have been trained to believe that realizing pleasure in the bedroom is common sense and easily attainable. That perspective leads us to see that our concern, misgivings, or mistakes are proof that you are sexually unacceptable and inept.

Pleasure rooted in intimacy isn't guaranteed. By creating an atmosphere in which communication can unfold, the emotional depth of a couple's sexuality is further deepened. A spirit of experimentation, intrigue, and shamelessness in the bedroom requires open lines of communication. This spirit of which we speak is like a deep-seeded spring running beneath and within every aspect of the marriage.

I remember having to work at our sexual relationship in the early years. Beyond the emotional hurdles, we didn't always know how to do what we wanted to do. If there isn't freedom to voice ignorance to your most trusted friend, then rest assured you will have problems on all levels of the relationship. Trust and intimacy must be cultivated.

As obvious as that may seem, many young couples struggle to shrug off the fantasy that intimacy in the bedroom is as natural as the physical act of intercourse itself. The most powerful sexual experiences are always rooted in the unrestrained intimacy of complete trust and disclosure, not the absence of tension. Every honest couple will admit that there is a learning curve in the bedroom. Whether it is learning simple techniques so as to enhance your time together or getting acquainted with your partner's fears, desires, or inhibitions, every couple enters the bedroom open to learn and grow.

Like all the other areas of the marriage, sexual intimacy won't grow in a sterile, mistake-free environment. The struggles and the ensuing tension in a relationship are opportunity for emotional and spiritual growth.

The mistakes made and the hurt feelings present are only a threat to the degree that a couple stops freely sharing grace. Only a vigilant, deliberate, and communicating couple can keep from the godless indifference.

Unfortunately, the images embedded in our imagination have impacted our feelings and choices. We are impatient and insecure people. Our unwillingness to explore and talk openly with each other reveals our desire for intimacy at the lowest possible personal cost. The rule of the day is risk as little as possible and get as much as possible. For proof of this commitment, one need only consider the ubiquitous pornography industry. The supply is largely due to a huge demand. The more of these images consumed, the more focused the search becomes for bargain-basement intimacy. It's a vicious and destructive cycle. It's easy to see how real intimacy is undermined. Few things are more subtle and damaging in the long haul to intimacy and trust in a relationship.

Freedom not only gives way to selfless expression, but it also sets the stage for humble interactions. Redemption gives way to extravagant lovemaking, which in turn thrives in a free and open atmosphere. Freedom changes our mind about conflict. Instead of being something to avoid, conflict is the cauldron in which beauty and intimacy are refined. By its very nature and design, sexuality is a tension-filled, intimate struggle in which life is celebrated and from which new life comes to be.

It is well documented that most couples experience difficulty in the area of sex.[8] Whether the struggles faced concern sexual desire, sexual arousal, orgasm, or overall satisfaction, the bedroom is an important crossroads in the life of a marriage. Just like in other areas within a marriage, a safe environment, open communication, the absence of shame, trust, and honesty will be critical.

The sexual intimacies couples are intended to enjoy become powerful forces of renewal and hope. For the couple who struggles well through difficulties, the bedroom will be a place of enjoyment and rest like no other place in their life. They will experience one of God's most amazing gifts. Far from a place of selfish demands, the bedroom becomes a place of otherworldly pleasure. Consider Solomon's unblushing enjoyment as recorded in the Song of Songs:

> *I went to my garden, dear friend, best lover!*
> *Breathed the sweet fragrance.*
> *I ate the fruit and honey,*
> *I drank the nectar and wine.*
> *Celebrate with me, friends!*
> *Raise your glasses—"To life! To love!"*[9]

DISCUSSION QUESTIONS:

1. Discuss the difference between sex being an end in and of itself and being an expression of something much deeper. What happens in a relationship (in and out of marriage) when this is confused?

2. Have you spent time talking with your partner about fear, shame, mistakes made in the area of sex?

3. Note Lisa's comment: If true love doesn't wait, true love forgives. What areas of your sexuality are you needing forgiveness in? Which areas are you needing peace and healing?

4. Discuss the importance of redemption, extravagance, and freedom in the sexuality of a marriage.

5. Discuss the idea that the sex life a couple also has in it a level of tension.

1. Song of Songs 7 (MES)

2. C.S. Lewis, *Weight of Glory*, 26.

3. Romans 1:21-2 (MES)

4. Mason, Mike, *The Mystery of Marriage* (Portland: Multnomah, 1985) 119.

5. Schaumburg, Harry W., *False Intimacy: Understanding the Struggle of Sexual Addiction*, (Colorado Springs: NavPress, 1992), 23.

6. Hirsch, Sharon, "The Desperation of God: A reflection of the feminine desire for relationship," *Mars Hill Review*: Fall 1997, p.28

7. Hosea 2:14-15 (MES)

8. Wincze, John P. and Carey, Michael P, *Sexual Dysfunction: A Guide for Assessment and Treatment* (New York: Guilford Press, 1991), 8.

9. Peterson, Eugene, *The Message Remix*, (NavPress, 2003), 1187.

"Every time one of my babies was about to be born, I'd think to myself, You're going to die! This time you're going to die! Then it'd come out. Somehow—I don't know how to explain it—but somehow it was like I had been born again."

—an Italian woman quoted in *Birthing From Within*

8. AN IMPORTANT CHOICE

To birth or not to birth, that is the question. And you
will hear many varied answers. Some will claim you
can never have children too soon or too many. Your
mother may offer a ransom for the first grandchild
born in the family. At times tension emerges when one
spouse is ready and the other is not. Trying to time the
birth of a child is like trying to hold back the seas. As
the Scriptures say, "God is sovereign over the womb."
Children will come at the right time and in the correct
number (unless you take the drugs that might make you
have seven babies at one time). On the other hand, there
are drugs that help you have no babies at all.

BIRTH CONTROL

These very words imply the impossible. Control over birth? It will never happen. The only thing more mysterious than sex (in marriage) is pregnancy and birth. So try as you may, do not live under any illusions. You have no control. But if you prefer to wait for children, it is important to consider your options of contraception. These are three of the most common forms of contraception:

MANY PEOPLE BELIEVE THE PILL AND IUD (INTRAUTERINE DEVICE) ARE ABORTIFACIENTS. DO YOUR OWN RESEARCH! —LS

The Pill—I would suggest a great deal of caution with birth control pills. The concept of injecting your body with foreign hormones is not to be approached lightly. For Lisa and I, it was disastrous. The side effects made our first year much

ACTUALLY, I WAS ON THE PILL ELEVEN YEARS (BETWEEN BABIES) AND LOVED IT. —MK

harder, and it took us some time to discover that "the pill" was a part of our problem. Not only was Lisa gaining weight and feeling miserable, it greatly reduced her libido and physical responsiveness to sex. For some women "the pill" seems to work well, but you must ask, "Is there a better way, and are the risks of side effects worth it?"

Plastic Things—Another option is to put plastic things in or on your privates. I have never been a big fan of this method either. Even the word latex is a major turn-off to me. The awkward pause during foreplay caused by fumbling around with a small latex object seems like working on a crossword puzzle during sex. Nonetheless, many couples maneuver the use of condoms and diaphragms with tremendous ease. Every married couple should try these at least once—the worst thing that can happen is you get a few laughs and you rule out latex and those uncomfortable trips to the drug store.

Natural Family Planning—I like most things that have the word nature in it. Think about it— natural food is always better than Twinkies or Little Debbie snacks full of chemicals and preservatives. The same goes for sex. Natural family planning is non-

LEARN THIS METHOD IF FOR NO OTHER REASON THAN TO BE BLOWN AWAY AT GOD'S CRE-ATIVITY WHEN HE DESIGNED THE FEMALE BODY. ONCE YOU GET TO KNOW YOUR BODY'S SIGNALS, YOU'LL REALIZE GOD GAVE YOU ALL THE SIGNS YOU NEED TO NE-GOTIATE TIMING WITHOUT HAV-ING TO TURN TO BODY-ALTERING DRUGS. —LS

toxic and free from additives and interruptions—pure, unadulterated sex. The basic philosophy of natural family planning is to chart your ovulation cycle so that you are aware of the days you may potentially impregnate your spouse. The ovulating days are days you want to stop on the ten-yard line or charge into the end-zone, depending on whether you would like a baby or not. But remember, we all make "mistakes," and when you do, make sure you have some form of health insurance.

PREGNANCY

A shocking day will come when the two of you will take a small stick into the bathroom. As you wait to see lines appear, you will get the most shocking news of your life. I wish I had been diligent enough to journal on these important days of my life. But journaling is something everyone says you should do, but no one really does. It just so happens that on January 31, 2003, I had been hired by Slate.com to keep a weeklong diary that would be posted daily on their web site. I had no idea at the time that the first day of this assignment would be one of these life-changing kind days. I wrote:

*I am a pastor, and that means I care for people. I am a
teacher/storyteller, spiritual director, friend, mentor, and a giver
of hope. I love it and am made for it. I had hoped to tell you
about a week of faithful service, as I counseled, encouraged,
and guided people that I love and care about. Yet it seems God
is not without a sense of humor. You might not see much of me
giving selflessly to others this week.*

*My wife, Lisa, 21-month-old daughter, Hanna, and I
went to dinner Saturday night with a friend. After introducing
him to Ninfa's (some of the best Tex-Mex you will ever taste),
I dropped them off and went to rent a movie and closed out
Saturday night on a relaxing note.*

*As I pulled into Hollywood Video, my Nextel phone
(which is like a two-way radio, but better) screamed, "YOUR
APARTMENT IS ON FIRE! COME HOME!" I
thought it was a joke, but it wasn't. I raced home. My wife
and baby were safe outside, but there was smoke everywhere,
and the smell of burnt plastic was putrid and pouring out the
door. I found a fire extinguisher encased in glass that would
not break. It must have been freakin' Plexiglas or something,
because it took twenty blows to shatter it. I ran into our
smoke-filled apartment to find a kitchen that is one big flame.
I empty four extinguishers. Neighbors keep bringing more
over just as I empty one. I can't see anything, so I just take a*

*deep breath, run in, and hope for the best. Breathe … Run
… Spray … Run … Repeat, until all the extinguishers are
empty. I get most of the blaze out before the fire department
arrives. But I suck in enough smoke to make me eligible for
clinical trials for people with high risk of lung cancer. The
firefighters convinced me to get some oxygen in the ambulance
while they finished fighting the flames.*

*Fire destroyed and smoke permeated everything. It left
nothing untouched. My family spent the night in an empty
apartment twenty blocks away and tried to sleep as we sorted
out the ramifications of cleaning or replacing everything we
owned and where we would live. Sleep mostly escaped me.
My mind focused on the joy of my "night-night" ritual with
Hanna at home. We all play in our bed, sing in the mirror,*

MY LIFE WAS FOREVER CHANGED
BY THE MIRACLE OF BIRTH. —LS

*read books, tickle each
other, and fade off to sleep
as a family. That routine seemed weeks or months away
from being reality again. So, my wife washed smoky clothes
all night, and we got ready for our church service on Sunday
evening (I know most churches meet in the a.m., but we are
not most churches. These young postmodern urban dwellers are
happy to sleep till noon and worship late). My wife sent me
to the store with a grocery list. It said: lemons (for a lemonade
fast so I could detox all the carcinogens that I swallowed last*

night), paper plates, cups, a knife, papaya, distilled water, soy milk, and a pregnancy test. I thought she was most likely paranoid that inhaling smoke and cleaning soot could endanger a potential fetus. If a $12 pregnancy test would put her mind at ease, then it was a worthwhile investment.

So we cut the papaya, drank some water, and took the test. Holy hellfire! There were two lines! Parents, you know what I'm talking about. There is a control line and a "You are great with child" line. Lisa was pregnant. We were going to have our second child; I am a father of a homeless family of four.

At 5:30, Ecclesia, our spiritual community, met for our quarterly love feast. It is a celebration of Christian community—a time to share our stories of joy and sorrow. A great crowd was there for music, cuisine, and real-life stories. I shared ours, and the community found ways to lighten our load. By the end of the night, we found out we had countless people coming over to clean, $90 had been collected to buy supplies, and friends were making us dinner each night of the week.

If I could have chosen a time for my wife to become pregnant, it would not be in the process of losing our apartment and possessions. We spent the following months sleeping on the floor at a friend's house as Lisa spent her days and nights vomiting (her favorite pregnancy activity). But the pain of that era in our life is but a distant memory. Nine months later, Trinity entered the world in a large bathtub as I gently caught her.

GOD'S GREATEST GIFT

Don't you see that children are God's best gift? The fruit of the womb his generous legacy?[1]

Having children will not fix your marriage; it will only amplify the current state of your union. It will give you an opportunity to come together in ways you never have before. Pregnancy is the beginning of the greatest journey of your lifetime. Your children will be the source of your greatest joy and at times your deepest sorrow. That is the nature of all things that are truly good. For Lisa and I, pregnancy, birth, and children have given us the most beautiful experiences of our life. When I saw the strength of my bride as she passionately persevered in ushering all three of my children into the world naturally, I was consumed with affection for her love and self-sacrifice. She became a different woman to me, and I love her more deeply than ever. These are some suggestions on how to walk this path together:

1) Men should take a prominent role in pregnancy, birth, and child-rearing. During the first trimester, men should begin by reading *Husband Coached Childbirth* by Dr. Bradley. Accompany her to doctor/midwife appointments and consider giving up alcohol and caffeine with your wife as your baby gestates.

2) Research everything you can about childbirth. You cannot rely on medical professionals to make decisions for you; this will be your baby and your birth.

3) Research and develop your philosophy of health and nutrition for your family. Your children need a healthy diet in the early years more

> WHEN I AM PRESENT AND FULLY EXPERIENCING THE MIRACLE OF BIRTH AND CHILDREN, I SEE THE FACE OF GOD MORE CLEARLY THAN EVER. NO WONDER I CAN'T GET ENOUGH OF IT. —LS

than any other time, yet many children eat a steady diet of fast food and fried chicken fingers. Don't be lazy; take some initiative and care for your children.

4) There are many philosophies about how to raise
   children; rest assured they can't train themselves.
   A couple must be in agreement about methods of
   discipline, attachment philosophy, values held within
   the home, and educational goals.

Explore the spirituality of birth through two of my
personal favorites: *Birthing from Within* by Pam England
and *The Naturally Healthy Pregancy* by Shonda Parker.

The God of the Bible is pro-children. The psalmist
sang, "He gives childless couples a family, gives them joy
as the parents of children."[2] Jesus was a child advocate
in His day. Throughout the Roman Empire, it was
common for children to be beaten, abused, and used
as slaves. In many cultures, including our own, people
espouse ideologies that view children as pests, carriers
of disease, or needless financial expenses. As with all of
Jesus' teachings, He turned the prevailing thought on its
head. Christ was often seen placing His hand on a child
and speaking a blessing. Though His disciples resented
this pattern, He said, "Let the little children come to
me, and do not hinder them, for the kingdom of heaven
belongs to such as these."[3]

Where some see obligation, expense, and duty, God offers blessings. Beware of the sinuous thoughts that degrade children. Our spiritual journeys are centered on abandoning our own selfishness for something greater. The strongest impulse in my life is no longer self-preservation; I would endure any pain or sacrifice to protect my children. With the birth of each of my children, I have become a better man; God has refined me and made me rich as He fills my home with love and laughter.

Be fruitful and multiply. It is not a suggestion; it is a command from the Holy Scriptures. God's people are to have children, train them in the ways of Christ and impact the world through offspring. Like much of the Old Testament, modern Christians have carefully selected the passages we want to keep and have thrown the rest aside. Scripture should never be inspiration for legalism (i.e. the teachings of the Pope and Mormon church on birth control) but lessons for life. The world will be a better place if we populate it with children who are taught the truths of historic Christianity. Emerging generations will reach out to all peoples with mercy, care for the earth, and tell the redemptive story of Christ beautifully. If we are to join Christ in praying that the kingdom of God "will come, on earth as it is in heaven," then we should supply the means to help get the job done.

DISCUSSION QUESTIONS:

1. What values and traditions do you want to pass on from your family of origin? Share some of your favorite memories from childhood.

2. Do you have friends with small children? What can you do to seek them out to learn from them?

3. Is there any history of child abuse in your family? Do you know families that have experienced this kind of trauma?

4. Commit together to read about birth, birth control, nutrition, and child raising together.

1. Psalm 127:3 (MES)

2. Psalm 113:9 (MES)

3. Matthew 19:14

"*Love is an earthquake that relo-cates the center of the universe.*"

—Mike Mason, *The Mystery of Marriage*

9. A FERTILE SOIL

Marriage thrives in the open air and rich soil of other relationships. Or, like the flower bed I toil over in my front yard, competitive roots and suffocating soil cause it to die. The impact friendships and family have on a marriage is significant and should not be underestimated. In this chapter we will consider the impact these relationships have on the marriage and how the couple must take responsibility for putting those relationships into the right perspective.

The Ceremony

It was an intimate, outdoor setting. The sky was gray,

evoking a serene, peaceful feeling. Our chairs were arranged on the side of a hill, which cascaded down into a nearby bayou snaking through sandy banks. Large pine trees surrounded the proceedings like guards standing watch over something very important. Even though we were in the shadow of a large metropolitan city, it felt like the wedding was removed a million miles. The pastor's words were easily heard without a microphone. There was a passionate plea easily seen in his eyes and heard in his voice. It was immediately obvious that he had walked closely with the eager couple standing before him. His demeanor, complemented by a funny quip here and there, put everyone at ease. This occasion was sacred, beautiful, and joy-filled.

His words stirred guests out of mere spectatorship and into an active role of supporting and encouraging the newborn marriage. I was reminded of the glut of wedding ceremonies that lack this connection. With the absence of rich symbolism, the pomp and circumstance point to little more than the amount of money poured into the decorations.

The size of weddings and the money spent on

extravagant decorations often lack any real significance to what is actually happening. Like so many other things in our consumer driven culture, the size and money spent at weddings are often equated with substance. If a couple spent as much thought and time to planning a ceremony that pointed to and captured the meaning of the covenant they, their friends, and their families were entering into, they would have started their relationship on solid footing. Careful consideration should be given to how the ceremony is a bridge that connects their separate lives—with all their family members and friends—with their future life of one flesh.

Ceremonies should point each person in attendance toward God. The very reason for such a gathering is God's idea in the first place. As we have said earlier, marriage is created for His glory. A God-centered orientation, then, should stir the hearts of family and friends into an intentional support system surrounding the newlywed couple. The symbolism and passages within the ceremony should capture the sense of vital transition and change. The combination of Western consumerism and individualism, however, makes this much-needed reality a rarity.

With fickle and selfish human nature, these unblushing promises of "till death do us part" and "for richer or poorer" are extravagant, to say the least. As one writer has observed, "They give away their freedom. They take on themselves each other's burdens. They bind their lives together in ways that are even more painful to unbind emotionally, humanly, than they are to unbind legally."[1] Given the extravagance embedded in the promises being made, one is left with little choice but to call marriage's designer, the Creator himself, into these proceedings.

Unfortunately, many ceremonies come off as either faddish or blind allegiances to tradition. Annie Dillard's observation about church attendees, such as those gathered at weddings, comes to mind, "Why do people in churches seem like cheerful, brainless tourists on a packaged tour of the Absolute?" She goes on to ask a pointed question, "Does anyone have the foggiest idea of what sort of power we so blithely invoke? Or, as I suspect, does no one believe a word of it?"[2]

For any number of reasons, couples blindly follow traditions or popular wisdom when planning a wedding.

The tension between what parents want and what the bride and groom want can be overwhelming. It can seem insurmountable, especially for a younger couple. Facing this tension and working through it, however, can be the first place in which the couple builds a new life together with the blessing of their parents. The ceremony honors the people who have had a hand in leading you to this juncture in your life. The ceremony also captures in its liturgy the reordering of life in light of this new relationship. The marriage takes the lead in priority and values over one's family and close friendships. The ceremony, then, highlights both the history leading up to that day as well as the future relationship and family taking root.

At Ecclesia we take seriously both the history a couple brings to the relationship and the future they are looking toward. We encourage members to take part in a special time set aside for spoken blessings. Instead of simply "showering" the couple with more trinkets, blessings are opportunities for engaged, newly married, or expectant couples to gather with close friends and family members. Guests arrive prepared to speak a blessing into the couple's life. Typically, a blessing involves the men gathering in one part of the house and the women in another.

One by one, the men and women go around their circles giving voice to experience, warning, encouragement, and honesty to the man and woman. Weddings and the birth of children are important rites of passage within Ecclesia. On more than one occasion, I have sat, tears running down my cheeks or laughing out loud as I listened to fathers, friends, or brothers speak powerful words into a loved one's lives. Each time I drive away, I'm deeply grateful for our community, as well as saddened that our culture (the Church included) has been swept away by merchandising and consumerism, giving gifts instead of speaking words of blessing.

Taken together, then, the blessings as well as the rehearsal and ceremony capture the spiritual and emotional reality: two different people from two different places beginning a journey to become one. The Church has rid itself of so much of its beautiful liturgy and symbol that most participants and couples getting married don't think of the ceremony as a canvas to depict God's design. The couple should work closely with the pastor overseeing the ceremony to keep this image at the forefront.

While seated at a reception of a wedding I had just performed, I struggled to understand my pastoral role. I sat quietly, away from the celebrants, alone with my thoughts. The sweltering summer evening pressed in on me as I struggled with an adequate image of my role. With the people dancing and eating, celebrating with the newlyweds, my homily in retrospect seemed to have only delayed what they rightfully wanted to do in the first place. The vows and the ceremony, by now thirty minutes old, echoed with drudgery and obligation. The thoughts swirled in my head, "Why didn't I just have them state their intention and bless them with a prayer? Did I really need to even be there?"

I eventually crawled out of my cave and joined in the celebration. I laughed and drank and met new friends. The question lingered, though. I returned to the hotel room with Meeka. I had felt this same feeling before when I spoke at commencements and other special occasions. In the drab, dark, and quiet motel room that night, the simple purpose came to me.

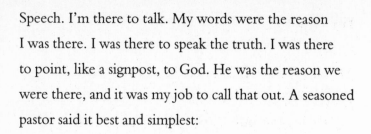

Speech. I'm there to talk. My words were the reason
I was there. I was there to speak the truth. I was there
to point, like a signpost, to God. He was the reason we
were there, and it was my job to call that out. A seasoned
pastor said it best and simplest:

> *"So why are we there? We are there to say God. We are there
> for one reason and one reason only: to pray. We are there to
> focus the brimming, overflowing, cascading energies of joy …
> if only for a moment but for as long as we are able, on God.
> We are there to say God personally, to say his name clearly,
> distinctly, unapologetically, in prayer. We are there to say it
> without hemming and hawing, without throat clearing and
> without shuffling, without propagandizing, proselytizing, or
> manipulating. We have no other task on these occasions."*[3]

Other symbols, passages, and rituals play in concert with
the pastor's words, pointing to the One who designed,
sustains, and ultimately blesses the marriage. All of
these "say God." Their place at the ceremony serves
as the beginning of the continual whisper echoing in
every corner of the marriage. Friends and family play a
powerful role in encouraging the couple to listen for that
still small voice in years to come.

THE FAMILY

My Big Fat Greek Wedding couldn't have provided a better glimpse into the sometimes tricky and much needed gracious attitude of bringing together two people and their families. The need for a sense of humor doesn't hurt either. Even if you weren't raised in a Greek family, chances are you could see familiar themes in the romantic comedy.

Most couples can appreciate the impact their family has had on preparing them for marriage. This appreciation, though, can range from a passing glance to an emotional prison. So much of that appreciation is directly related to your personal experience in growing up, the kind of family you had, and your parents' relationship.

Try as we may, our family's mark is indelible. Turning and facing the legacy,

SPEND SOME WEEKNIGHTS WATCHING THIS AND OTHER WEDDING FILMS TOGETHER. IT WILL OPEN THE DOOR TO SOME GREAT DISCUSSIONS. —CS

both the good and bad, must be undertaken, not only before you are married, but well into the first few years of marriage. Ideas and images assumed at an early age lie

dormant and undetected in our minds until we begin
to struggle within marriage. Unpacking the family bags
for the very first time four or five years in to a marriage
presents an incredible challenge for the "happiest"
of couples. The ramifications can be devastating and
protracted.

This "unpacking" is more than objectively learning
about your future in-laws as though they were strange
specimens from another planet. You must see your new
family from the inside-out. Share meals and stories
with your future father and mother-in-law. Visit with
your brother and sister-in-laws. Avoid the posture of
analyzing and diagnosing what you see as the eccentricity
in your new family. If you happen to see things that
give you reason for concern, look for undistracted
settings and productive times in which to talk with your
fiancé or your spouse. Don't allow the dysfunction of
family members to discourage your efforts to know one
another.

Within the home, the mother and father relationship
acts as a relational climate control. Each one of us
grows up in different climates, shaped and influenced

differently. In my experiences in premarital as well as marriage counseling, the families with "obvious" problems are too often considered at the expense of the more subtle, but no less profound, impact of the so called "normal" upbringing. Don't be fooled into thinking that one's upbringing was hopeless while the other was perfect. The lingering effects are delayed much of the time. Months, years, decades can go by before certain traits come to light. Likewise, a couple should not see their history as fates sealed in granite. Through redemptive lenses, a couple comes to see their heritage as part of God's larger story.

As your past relationships begin to meet your engagement or your marriage, the soil is ripe for shame and self-contempt or for division in your marriage. It is natural to feel protective of friends and family, even though you may know them to be wrong. It's a very delicate and uneasy feeling to begin opening up to the person you love about the relationships that have impacted you. Rejection is a looming risk.

Every fiber in you may want to carefully and tediously manage how your story comes out; by holding back and sharing only bits and pieces, you wrongfully think you are able to control what your spouse thinks of you, thus minimizing the risk. While understandable on the one hand, an overly protective posture will surely undermine the trust and intimacy you could forge with your spouse during these difficult times. It's paradoxical. The path to a more satisfying relationship crosses painful territory. The communication and the shared wisdom of a spouse lessen the likelihood of past sins governing future relationships with spouse and children. As the Proverb says, "You can't whitewash your sins and get by with it; you find mercy by admitting and leaving them."[4]

Two things occur when we open up. One, you build a deeper and more intimate relationship with your spouse. Secondly, open communication disrupts dysfunctional relational patterns that thrive and grow in secrecy. The piercing presence of your partner seems imposing and unconformable, but in the end is a means by which God redeems your story, making something good out of what you thought hopelessly shameful.

The context for such a dialogue is a sturdy, trustworthy love. The love of a spouse creates a safe environment for facing the sometimes harsh and familiar realities of family history. Likewise, very few things are more disappointing than to have your spouse stand in judgment or show contempt for your family. To tread into the waters of past sins or family history may be more than you believe your spouse or fiancé can handle. Sometimes these difficult conversations must take place with a pastor, elder, or a trusted counselor. If truth and grace is what a couple seeks, then God will be faithful, giving wisdom to navigate the narrow passages of family history. The wisdom of God clarifies the difference of what it means to remain connected without being governed by one's family.

An ongoing, healthy relationship and perspective into each other's family is a crucial part of a strong foundation in marriage. In our fragmented and isolated culture, staying connected with family members and with each other's family heritage is difficult but important. The stories that make up family history can be stories of hope and redemption instead of death sentences and reasons for cynicism. I'm reminded of the Psalm in which David proclaims as one who has seeing with wisdom from God:

Even the darkness will not be dark to you;
the night will shine like the day,
for darkness is as light to you.[5]

Friends

Friendships, like family, figure prominently into a
healthy marriage. A couple would do well, whether
they live near family or not, to nurture and cultivate
friendships that will underscore the sacred vows they
have spoken.

Up until just a few years back, I shared a cup of coffee
every week for four years with two men, one ten years
and the other twenty years older than myself. We met
every Wednesday morning from 6:30 to about 8 a.m.
We came together because we were friends. We enjoyed
each other's company. We were three men struggling
to make sense of our faith. Pushed and pulled by the
demands in the world, we struggled to maintain a
healthy balance in our life. We weren't gathered around
Bible study or early hours of prayer. While I knew these
men to be men who were being influenced by Scripture,
men who prayed for me, we gathered together to give

to and take strength from one another. Our time was less about "accountability" wherein we reported our misbehavior, and more about focusing on visions of what it meant to be honest and real men who led their families. I came away stronger. Meeka and our children benefited from their influence in my life. Those sleepy Wednesday mornings are a priceless part of my spiritual and relational development.

Our wives spent time together, too. We gathered in each other's homes; we celebrated special occasions and mourned tragedies together. We spoke life-giving words to each other's children. We worshiped together, learned together, and struggled together. Their friendship was (and continues to be) a refuge and a place where we were invited to live honest and authentic lives. Much of what is honorable in my marriage God fashioned through these friendships.

Meeka and I were just starting out, where they were in the middle years of their life together. We were young and full of idealism, just beginning to have children. Their years of experience were an asset to us. They were (are) gracious to allow us to hang out with them. As

Meeka and I are now three kids and several years further down the road, we relish opportunities to lend young couples a hand in their relationship. We intend to give to them what was given to us. We intentionally invite them over during dinnertime, gathering at the table with us and our three children. We open our home to them, allow them a glimpse of our life. It is a powerful form of pre-marital counseling.

In fact, we will often have couples looking forward to marriage bring over a list of questions for us. We have them make a list of five or so questions about being married. One particular couple recently brought the following questions:

- *What has been the most significant struggle you have faced as a couple?*
- *What would you point to as the most glorious aspect of your marriage?*
- *What does headship and submission look like in real life?*
- *What did you not know going into marriage that you know now and wish you would have known then?*

Marriage, by its very nature, is a fluid, organic, and

unscientific adventure. It is, as we saw in chapter one, rooted in the character of God. Doling out advice in a sterile counseling office, though popular, is often of very little practical help to a couple. An environment that is active and open but trusted and grounded in faith can be even more helpful to a couple looking forward to marriage vows. Sadly, the culture that surrounds most marriages in the West fosters unhealthy independence, walled off from any meaningful contact except to call in the professionals. And even when professional help is reasonable and needed, this shouldn't be sought after in isolation.

The same isolated and fragmented culture that divides couples from their family heritage convinces them to live independently of close friends. The message pervading the human situation convinces us to secure our home, marriage, job, and over-all situation in life independently of anyone else—family or otherwise. Once our position is secured, conventional wisdom convinces us that friendships become a luxury, but are certainly not necessary. This lie runs contrary to the essence of our existence. Relationships are not an accessory, but are absolutely essential to the journey in this life. Friendships, single or with other married couples, become one of the most gracious, humbling, encouraging gifts God makes available to a couple. The power friends have in shaping our lives makes their integrity all the more important. Choose your friends wisely!

You can't choose your family, but you certainly can choose your friends. As powerful for good as a friendship can be, it can be equally damaging. Beyond the obvious and extreme like an affair, unhealthy friendships can subtly shift a spouse from a God-centered and open relationship, to one that is selfish and full of deceit. An emotional bond that exists in a relationship fuels the strength of ideas and images that come as a result of that relationship. One must be alert and aware of ideas and images being shared within a friendship. This becomes especially important when a couple is struggling. Reaching out for help isn't a guaranteed support.

Relationships that consistently distract a partner from the marriage will slowly and subtly create a disconnection. The couple will soon be faced with bridging a daunting crevice between them. While it may feel like it happened overnight, that feeling is merely indicative of the systemic problem that existed in the relationship to begin with. Seemingly overnight, you will be forced to choose between the marriage and a friendship. Instead of waiting until it's all but too late, make that decision every day and look forward to the support and encouragement of your friendships and families who will, even in your weakness and hurt feelings, esteem your marriage, pointing you back into the struggle with your spouse.

Relationships with friends and family, as well as a community of faith, are rich soil for a couple first starting out. The ceremony I described at the beginning of this chapter took place in Houston. Ours is a sprawling and frantic city; people commute hours and hours a week between work and home. For many, family and friendships are a weekend luxury.

That ceremony I told you about at the outset of this chapter took place in a remote, quiet corner of our city, just outside of downtown. For two or three hours that afternoon, the bride and groom enjoyed the celebration and attention of their friends and family. Dinner and dancing followed the ceremony, as did toasts and laughter. Each guest was there to support and encourage the newlyweds as a busy city roared past us. As I drove away from this oasis, I thought about the image it presented.

Though distractions were just outside the gate, it was clear why we had gathered there that afternoon. It was a sacred and communal gathering deserving our attention, even if only a few hours. Similarly, every marriage is surrounded by demands, cynics, and distractions that at best are indifferent to the marriage vows and at worst hostile. It will take the hard, deliberate work of every couple to make the primacy of their wedding vows with people who love them to enjoy a love that lasts a lifetime.

DISCUSSION QUESTIONS:

1. Ceremonies should point people ultimately toward God. How is this different than what most people expect of ceremonies?

2. How can a ceremony highlight both the couple's history and the future they are looking forward to?

3. What do you feel is important for your pastor to speak at your wedding? Assist him in finding certain areas of emphasis in his homily.

4. Other than language, what other truths do you want to capture at your ceremony through the ceremony itself?

5. Plan an evening to watch a movie centered around a wedding. Start with *My Big Fat Greek Wedding*. What are some other movies you can think to watch together? What truths or points of interest would be worth exploring that were present in the film that you viewed?

6. What sins are present in your family that threaten to enter into your new family? Are you willing to talk openly about your family? Can you talk freely with your spouse? Are you overly critical of your spouse's family?

7. Who is an older couple to whom you and your partner can approach and bring five or so questions about marriage? Make that list together and seek those people out.

8. What relationships are you currently in that distract,

undermine, or create unnecessary tension within your marriage?

1. Buechner, Frederick, *Whistling in the Dark: A Doubters Dictionary* (HarperCollins: San Francisco, 1993), 86-87.

2. Dillard, Annie, *The Annie Dillard Reader*, (HarperPerennial: New York, 1994) 38.

3. Peterson, Eugene, *Subversive Spirituality*, (Eerdamans: Grand Rapids, 1994) 150.

4. Peterson, Eugene, *The Message Remix*, (NavPress, 2003), 1147.

5. Psalm 139

Don't use the "S" Word!

CONCLUSION

We began this book by looking into the vision of marriage because we believe the order to be of most importance. If you are engaged, newly married, or even contemplating taking the next step in a relationship, chapter two in this book should be read and studied closely. You should seek the counsel of older and wiser people about marriage; sit down and talk with the veterans. I (Chris) recently visited with a couple married for more than fifty years that were choosing to separate from one another. No matter how deep your affection or Christian devotion, marriage is never easy and cannot be put on automatic pilot. Love your God and your neighbor (your spouse should be your most critical neighbor).

But even as you do that, you should know that a marriage that is true to the Christian vision is possible insofar as two people commit to live sacrificially and unselfishly first before God and second with each other. Thus chapter two must be taken into serious consideration. The romance will fade, and something more sustainable and courageous must grow in its place.

As abstract as some of this may sound, though, daily decisions, seemingly invisible and understated are the bricks upon which a home is built. Don't get lost in your ideals and with psychological principles that don't foster awareness and simplicity in your relationship. The battle, if you will, is won or lost in the most mundane and regular decisions.

We have offered our insight and our wives' feedback as a balance and connection to our very real lives and struggles as husbands. While writing this book, I was most aware of the fact that I am no marriage expert. Our wives have been our most faithful teachers, fellow strugglers, and lovers. God has used these women more consistently and powerfully to draw out of us the weak, insecure, and corrupt only to install His faith, hope, and love. And this continues to this day.

Enter the marriage vows with a community of people who will share your commitment and child-like willingness to learn and grow for the rest of your life. Take what God has created with the utmost seriousness while not losing your sense of humor and adventure. Inflexibility and hardheadedness undermine a marriage like no other traits.

Marriage carries with it the redemptive force to make you a different person—and not for the reasons that you think. A life lived to please one's self is empty, and the journey to become one will finally lead you to empty yourself for the sake of one another—unlike dating, which feeds on our consumerist tendencies to get what we want and indulge ourselves. The dirty secret of dating is that it centers on a game of power. Courtship is too often about control. One person is falling in love faster and relinquishing power to the other. So the game is all about pacing, being honest and open—but never revealing too much. This dance is deceptive and self-serving. As you approach the altar, leave your dating life behind and embrace the new rhythms of marital life.

The nature of this new lifestyle is about service and submission. Submission has become a dirty secret of the Christian Scriptures—no one wants to talk about it. There are dozens of books on marriage attempting to pave a nuptial path without submission. The question makes sense, "How can I marry and still choose my own trail?" You cannot. Becoming one means you give yourself to one another without holding back. If you are a person of Christian faith, submission should already be a part of your lifestyle, but it likely is not. Who should I submit to?

Believers

Christian community is a source of strength, encouragement, and security. Many choose to receive selectively from their church, taking what they want and avoiding the rest. I have seen too many individuals and families that run from the people who know them the best. God will surround you with trustworthy people of faith if you seek out Christian community.

Authorities

We must submit to the laws of the land and the people who have authority over us. Submission is not simply about obedience. Honoring your parents may mean continuing to submit to them on issues that are not destructive to your new family or contradictory to your faith.

Your Spouse

Wives are to submit to husbands and husbands are to submit to their wives. Nothing is clearer in Scripture. Good marriages are marked by mutual submission. If you find yourself contemplating your rights and what you are entitled to from your spouse, then you are missing the whole point of marriage. Give yourself away and reap the benefits in intimacy, sex, finances, and faith. Blessings on your journey!

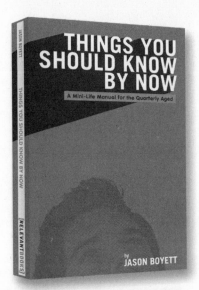